the Naughty Girl's Guide to Life

SPHERE

First published in Great Britain in 2007 by Sphere
Reprinted 2007 (Twice)

Text copyright © Tara Palmer-Tomkinson and Sharon Marshall 2007
Illustrations by Robyn Neild
Design by D.R. ink

The moral right of the author has been asserted.

A CIP catalogue record for this book
is available from the British Library.

ISBN 978-1-84744-137-9

Printed and bound in Italy by LEGOSpA

Sphere
An imprint of
Little, Brown Book Group
100 Victoria Embankment
London EC4Y 0DY

An Hachette Livre UK Company

www.littlebrown.co.uk

the Naughty Girl's Guide to Life

TARA PALMER-TOMKINSON
AND SHARON MARSHALL

sphere

WE'D LIKE TO DEDICATE
THIS BOOK TO OUR
ADORING HUSBANDS,
WITHOUT WHOM IT JUST
WOULDN'T BE POSSIBLE.

Only kidding.

INTRODUCTION:

Naughty

and *proud* of it

Naughty:
(pronounced naw-tee)

Adjective: naugh·ti·er, naugh·ti·est

Adv: naugh' ti·ly

Full of mischief, disobedient, scandalous, saucy, risqué

The sort of girl who's always having a *really* good time

Thank you for buying this book. We're both saving for boob jobs and you have just made a *very* valuable contribution. If you borrowed it, that's OK. You may be skint. Or traumatised because you've been dumped. We'll still help. If you stole it from someone's handbag, put it back, you thieving cow. She was reading it.

For the rest of you, we're going to need you to sit down and concentrate. You know, there's so much more you can be getting away with in life. There's no need to be so *nice*. Nice is not that nice. Life is soooo much better when you're naughty.

There was a time when we thought life sucked. Men have broken our hearts. We've had really lousy flatmates. We've worked for absolute swines. Sharon got so fat through sulking she ended up doing a TV dieting show. Tara got so thin, the paparazzi needed magnifying glasses to find her.

We've been at our lowest ebb. We've even worn flat shoes. And tights. Boil-washed woollen tights. But it was time to pull our stockings up.

Two victims became two vixens.
We got naughty.

We've worked out how to skive off work for weeks on end and yet still have the boss believe you're an absolute hero. We've figured out how to ensure our love life is so much better than our flatmates'. We learnt the perfect undressing technique to convince your new lover that you're not really flat-chested.

Forget the twelve steps to recovery. We've gone straight to step thirteen – the naughty step. Bye-bye Miss Goody Two-Shoes. Hello Miss Sh*g Me Shoes and Stockings.

We can't remember what it's like to be good any more. And the thing is, we're getting away with it. You can too.

It's time you learnt the tips. By reading this you're now an official member of the naughty club. Here's how to get up, get out and get over all that life can throw at you. Plus how to get your own back on those that deserve it.

We won't teach you how to get away with murder. But we do want you to stay on top and in your killer heels.

Come on girls.* It's time to be super naughty.

---

* Boys are welcome too – although you can probably skip most of the advice on hosiery. (Yes, OK, we know some of you won't.) But if you feel like joining our club then follow our guide and we reckon you'll be getting a darn good spanking before you reach the end.

Frequently Asked
Questions

PART ONE:

The Naughty Girl in Love

PRAYER

Grant me the serenity to accept that singledom does not always suck

Courage to realise the search for Mr Right may well reach double figures

And the wisdom to know that even if that ex-lover list hits treble figures, you're not a slag.
You're just unlucky.

The Naughty Girl's Guide to Living Happily Ever After with Mr Right

This section is a bit shorter than the rest. That's because we wrote this book shortly after we both got dumped, so we've yet to find Mr Right. We're having lots of fun looking, though, and we've got some fabulous dating advice coming up later. But first, let us tell you what to do when it all goes wrong.

For the mere price of this book you've just bought your road to recovery. A fraction of what they charge for rehab. And we'll let you have a drink.

So sling on your Louboutins, pour yourself a lychee Martini,* settle back and learn the rules.

Most of the advice is legal.

---

* Incidentally, if you are in rehab, then well done and keep it up. Whenever we say alcohol, we mean a slice of chocolate cake for you.

The Naughty Girl's Guide to Living Happily Ever After When Mr Right Has Buggered Off

OK, let's start with the biggie. It's going to take us several pages. But stick with us because we're going to deal with how to survive getting dumped.

This is the finishing school of how to finish things. Except we ask you to read us, rather than walk about with the book on your head.

If you're one of those girls who always has a mature conversation with your ex in which you both sit down, conclude you're not quite right for each other, hug, then agree to stay the bestest of friends for ever, you can piss off. That's just showing off. This is a home for the bewildered.

First, let's start with a serenity prayer for the situation. We've sort of adapted it from AA – but added in alcohol.

> *Grant me the serenity to accept the jerk has gone for good,*
> *Courage to embrace my facial hair (because it will sprout*
> *through in times of trauma),*
> *And the wisdom to know that buying ten pairs of new shoes and*
> *sinking a large vodka really is a valid solution.*

How to Tell if You've Been Dumped Already

One of the problems with men is that sometimes they don't actually mention that you've been dumped. You're sort of left to figure it out.

Men just aren't as confrontational as women. Rather than just saying it's over, they think they're being soooo nice by just drifting gently out of your life. The trick is to spot the signs, so you can avoid all the drifting, get rid of the little loser and get straight down to being naughty with somebody else.

So, first of all, here are the signs.

CHECKLIST

❑ *Have those cosy conversations about how you must meet the parents/have lots of his babies/be blissfully happy for ever dried up?*

❑ *Has he suddenly come over all Donald Trump – claiming he can't see you because of endless 'business meetings'? (If he's started combing his hair like Donald's too, you really must end things immediately.)*

❑ *Is he now always texting you rather than calling?*

❑ *Is he always in a hurry to hang up? Claiming he's 'on the tarmac and about to take off/on a train/about to go into a tunnel' when you call? Ask yourself if this sudden spurt of jetsetting really fits his job – e.g. does Burger King really insist on all this international travel for its chefs?*

❑ *When you get serious on the telephone he says 'you're breaking up'. And deep down you know what he means is 'we're breaking up'.*

❑ *If you text him saying you want to ride him till dawn, does he come back with a message about his accountant/mother?*

❑ *Does he only ever call you and suggest meeting when he's either drunk or the pubs are shut?*

❑ *Now you think about it, does he look a bit sheepish all the time?*

❑ *Has he called you to say you need 'to talk'?*

❑ *Is he always having a shower before he gets home from late night meetings with 'the boss'?*

❑ *Is he just being too, well, sweet? Surprise flowers and gifts all the time? If it's out of the blue or out of character it could be out of guilt, you know.*

- ❏ *Does he look nothing like the Adonis he should do, given the number of hours he's spending at the gym?*
- ❏ *Does he always claim the scratches on his back came from a friend's cat, but it's pretty obvious the cat is about 5ft 7? And probably blonde.*
- ❏ *Is he claiming a headache when that should be your prerogative?*
- ❏ *Or – and this is always a bit of a giveaway – you haven't heard from him for weeks now?*

If most of this is looking a bit familiar then, girlfriend, you're about to be chucked. In fact, we hate to break the news to you, but you've probably been chucked already.

Exit with dignity. If you're still clinging to that last vestige of hope that the relationship might survive, you could go down the route of trying to play games. Try to look really busy in the hope he'll be intrigued and phone you to find out what you're up to. Switch the phone off so you look like you're doing something important. Get seen out with male friends. Get yourself into *OK!* magazine and trumpet your romance with someone else. Better still, announce it in Forthcoming Marriages in the *Telegraph*. That sort of thing.

But most of the time it's just easier to ask what's going on.

In your heart of hearts, when you know, you know. Go with your instincts and brace yourself. It hasn't worked out.

SOD HIM.

Face-to-Face Dumping

So, he's said those four little words:

1) We
2) Need
3) To
4) Talk

You're about to become a single woman again. Look on the bright side: at least he's been gentlemanly enough to let you know it's happening. Until she learnt the naughty rules, Sharon once had no idea things had ended until she received a text announcing his engagement to someone else. Tara once got engaged and didn't realise she wasn't his only fiancée until a Parisian newspaper exclusive revealed an identical engagement ring on another trusting and unsuspecting beauty's finger, announcing her engagement to the very same groom-in-waiting.

The most important thing now is that you take control. This is how you deal with it.

Arrange to meet face-to-face in three days' time. It will make you look busy/important and crucially gives you time to shop. Remember, in a dumping situation you're dressing for you, but also to say 'f*** you' to the man who is idiotic enough to leave you.*

---

* Incidentally, we think it's outrageous that the publisher made us put all these asterisks in the naughty words. We're in crisis. What do you mean, we can't even f***ing swear?

STYLE TIPS

Do not wear anything less than killer couture. Or at least a darn good rip-off from one of the better high street stores.

Avoid patterns, they could distract him. He needs to stay focused on you and how fabulous you are. Your strategy is to claw back a little self-respect by leaving him wishing he could have just one last assault of your body. Do not let him. This is one moment where demand should definitely exceed supply.

And girls, you've *got* to wear stockings.

Whether he sees them or not you're going to walk differently and feel differently. You cannot function on a full gusset. And no girl feels sexy and confident sweating in sixty denier.

Men like a bum, a waist and a cleavage on their women. If you look like an ironing board with your bra off, buy some 'chicken fillets' (no, not the ones that come in packets of two or four from the local deli). They're available from most department stores at the very reasonable price of forty pounds – cheaper by far than a boob job and just as convincing. Well, certainly while you've got all your clothes on.

Don't shove socks down there, they tend to look lumpy. If you need added help to achieve that hour-glass figure you crave, get a pair of heavily armoured girdle knickers. These go under the rather sexy name of Spanx at Harvey Nichols. Yes, OK, they sort of ruin all the work you're doing with the sexy stockings but they do make you look and feel much thinner. Most importantly, knowing you're constrained by those massive stomach-hugging, bum-squeezing, passion-killing garments of torture should ensure that you don't succumb to a final fling with him and ruin everything.

Choosing the right location
is vital. We suggest an Italian
restaurant as the waiters can be guaranteed to
flirt with you. If you can find the time, drop in the night
before, tip generously when you leave and you can then rely on
being greeted with cries of pleasure when you return for war. Be
certain to arrive late so he can witness the deep joy your presence
brings. And make him have to pretend to check his phone messages
for half an hour while he waits for you to show up. Waiting always
put him at a disadvantage. It won't make the slightest bit of

difference to whether you get dumped or not but it will make you feel soooo much better.

As soon as you arrive, order an expensive drink. A 1961 Château Latour is nice. You may as well have one final assault on his wallet.

Start talking immediately. Dive in. This avoids the torture of him bleating on about his work issues for half an hour until he musters up the courage to announce it's all over. We recommend you say something like this, 'Look. I don't think things are brilliant – maybe we should cool it?'

You can tell immediately by his reaction what the situation is. If he's clearly fighting the urge to holler with relief or actually starts shouting, 'Yes, Yes!', then we're sorry but that's it, girlfriend.

Once it's clear you're there to collect your dating P45, leave.

Do not cry. Do not beg. Excuse yourself and walk out of the front door. Leave him and the bill. Do not look back.

(Unless, of course, he chases after you, sobbing, saying you've completely misunderstood everything and, vitally, proposing marriage, in which case we would be prepared to make an exception.)

Take your little stocking-clad legs and gorgeous body home, pour yourself a drink and move straight on to page 34 where we'll tell you what to do next.

CHECKLIST

Read this through before you leave the house. Obey these rules. We want you graduating from our finishing school with your head held high, and knees together, while he's tortured with doubts about whether or not he's done the right thing.

- ❏ *If dumped, do not let him have that one last moment of passion with you. You look fabulous in your perfect outfit. It'll only crease if it ends up on his floor.*
- ❏ *Don't stay, cradling the remains of your wine, sharing your miserable history with the waiters.*
- ❏ *Do not go off with one of the waiters.*
- ❏ *It is, however, perfectly fine to accept the telephone number of the proprietor on your way out. After all you're a single girl now.*

NB: If he insists he wants to do the dumping at your home, then pop out to Harvey Nicks the day before, buy a pair of designer knickers and leave them lying on the floor – next to two half-empty glasses of wine. You may as well have the pleasure of keeping him guessing.

Being Dumped By Telephone

It's rare to find a man who agrees to share his airspace with you to let you know it's over. Most can't even be bothered to mention that your loving relationship has ended. They just sort of disappear leaving you to figure it out. In these situations we suggest you go for our one phone call, two texts rule. It saves time.

Let us explain.

You call. He doesn't pick up. You leave a nice friendly message to which any reasonable, sane, normal male would respond by calling you back that evening. He doesn't call.

OK. Leave it four days. Now you're officially entitled to send another message. Text in case your shaking voice betrays you or you feel the need to scream obscenities down the phone. Make the text flirty. Confident. Not in any way betraying the fact that you

Step one, pour yourself a very large Martini. Step two, switch your mobile to the screened calls setting where your caller ID isn't displayed, or use a landline that withholds its number. Call the bastard until he answers.

are terrified he's dumped you without even having the decency to alert you to the fact. No pressure. Throw in a line about how fabulously busy you are and isn't life just fun, fun, fun?

Nothing? Leave it another twenty-four hours. Still nothing? OK, the little s*** has definitely dumped you. Face it. He's not dead, his phone hasn't been stolen and he hasn't been kidnapped by aliens who are preventing him making that one last phone call home to his beloved.

It's up to you what you do next. Some girls can simply rise above it all and move on. Well done them. Personally, we prefer to make sure we have the last word. It's not textbook ladylike behaviour, but it does make us feel better.

Step one, pour yourself a very large Martini. Step two, switch your mobile to the screened calls setting where your caller ID isn't displayed, or use a landline that withholds its number. Call the bastard until he answers.

One day, eventually, finally, he'll pick it up. It's then your choice what you do next. Personally, we think that if you've been seeing him for longer than three months you're owed an explanation. Ask for it. This is probably the last conversation you'll have with him anyway, so stay in control, don't cry but let him know exactly what a pathetic unchivalrous swine he is. We've enjoyed phrases such as, 'I hope someone else appreciates your toothpick,' 'I thought you were more of a man,' 'I always had to pretend I was with someone else.' Occasionally, if appropriate, you could throw in, 'What a shame.' Please restrict the screaming insults to after you have put down the telephone, having made doubly sure it is switched off.

If you can't face the conversation then just send a text. Say you're 'disappointed in him that he didn't even have the gallantry to end the relationship'. He won't come back, but you can bet the little heel will read it.

If you want to save the cost of the call then use this fabulous tip, which was given to us by one TV gardener. They found Sharon sulking over a man and suggested she simply got her revenge by going round to his house at night and writing 'F*** you' in weed-killer on the lawn.

CHECKLIST

❏ *While waiting for his calls it is acceptable to pace the floor, chain-smoke, take four baths to help you relax, cry, let your stomach churn, spend hours staring at the phone, pour your heart out to your friends and repeatedly re-read his old texts for any clues of just when and why he changed his mind about you. All of this is perfectly normal.*

❏ *It is unacceptable to tearfully ring him in the middle of the night and demand to know why he doesn't love you. Do that and we'll be very disappointed. In fact, if you do we might just come round and instruct you to wear flat shoes for the rest of your life as punishment.*

The point of this chapter is to let you figure out what's going on as quickly as possible. Spot the signs. Act on your instinct. Find out what you're dealing with.

Then move on. You need to be **over him and under someone else** as soon as possible. We need you back in the saddle, girls. Don't worry, we've been through the whole thing. We know exactly what to do and we've written it all down for you.

How to Gauge if You're Being a Complete Psycho

OK. We'd like to take a moment to pause. Think. Assess. You've been dumped. How well are you handling it? Ideally, you'll be sitting there thinking that you're a sophisticated, modern-day woman who understands that life isn't a bed of roses and not all love is requited.

But we know that's unlikely. If you've done/are considering doing any of the following, we're extremely cross with you.

❑ *You've looked at his photograph.*   Yes/No
    (This is just about acceptable. He'll never know.)

❑ *You've been crying over his photographs.*   Yes/No
    (OK, he won't know, but it's time to pull yourself together.)

❑ *You're obsessively turning over in your head*
    any occasion he ever mentioned another woman,
    and wondering if he's with her.   Yes/No
    (Well, at least you're doing it in private. But you
    really need to snap out of this.)

❑ *You've been listening obsessively to that last*
    voicemail message of his.   Yes/No
    (Oh, just give us the phone so we can delete it.
    You'll drive yourself mad.)

❑ *You've sold the story of your 'heartache' to a*
    tabloid newspaper.   Yes/No
    (OK, but we would have preferred a glossy. We just
    hope you got a fair price for it. See page 246 for tips.)

❑ *You've phoned him after that last 'you've been dumped'*
    conversation, begging him to change his mind.   Yes/No
    (That's the limit. You're starting to look desperate.
    It's not as if he was Brad Pitt.)

❑ *You phoned a friend of his. To beg for their help to get him back.*   Yes/No

(Oh for goodness' sake, girl!)

❑ *You phoned his mother.*   Yes/No

(You're boring us now. We might have to get you sectioned.)

❑ *You've been loitering outside his home, looking at his bedroom window.*   Yes/No

(No, no, no. We are not happy with you. Do not go there again. You should be loitering in your own bedroom. With someone else.)

❑ *You're wearing woollen tights.*   Yes/No

(Get a grip.)

❑ *You're wearing flat shoes.*   Yes/No

(We give in.)

Pour yourself a tot of vodka, then tot up how many times you ticked 'Yes'.

(0–2)   *The Good.* Well done. Have you read us before or something? Now get your little butt over to page 83 and let's get you a new man.

(3–11)   *The Bad.* Girlfriend, you're not taking this well. Let us be frank, you're turning into one of those monstrous stalking-weeping-psycho-bitches-from-hell. You're in danger of going from Great to Glenn Close. The only way to emerge with your sanity, dignity, and clothes-sense intact, is to work your way through the rest of this book. Come back to this list when you've finished. We want you with a perfect score. And gusset-free.

The Naughty. Oh, as if you've got time to do a quiz. You're far too busy seducing your ex's father.

Crap Dumping Lines

Look, you feel crap but you're not the only girl in the world that's been through this, you know. To prove it, here is a selection of dumping lines we and our girlfriends have experienced.

We bet your guy's excuse came under one of these categories:

CHECKLIST

❏ *It's not you. It's me.*

❏ *I'm not good enough for you. (Incidentally – if you're ever given either of these lines you should agree with him wholeheartedly.)*

❏ *I need some space. (Offer to book him on an astronaut's course.)*

❏ *Things are so difficult at work. (Here we go, he's gone all Donald Trump again.)*

❏ *The timing just isn't right. (Yes, well, you'd noticed in bed that something was wrong with his timing.)*

❏ *I never got over my ex. (Offer to lend him this book – after all you'll be over him before the cab drops you back home.)*

❏ *I'm just not ready for a serious relationship.*

❏ *I need to learn to love myself before I can love anyone else.*

❏ *My mother didn't like you/thought you were such a slut. (Hmmm, OK maybe you shouldn't have slept with his father.)*

❏ *I can't bond with your dog/cat/armadillo/parrot.*

❏ *I only agreed to the OK! wedding for the cheque. (Yeah, well you only did it for the frock.)*

❏ *I've found someone else.*

❑ *I'm gay. (No, you can't have the frock.)*
❑ *I'm married.*
❑ *I hate it when you do Bruce Forsyth impressions in bed.*

Actually that last one was one *we* used on a man, but we include it as an example of how much more original and imaginative us women can be compared to men who simply churn out the same old excuses. Face it, if he can't even be bothered to come up with a decent reason for ending things, why let him get to you?

Men are pretty predictable creatures, so the best thing a girl can do is to trust her instincts. But it's always worth confronting the man if you have a problem. There could be a perfectly reasonable explanation for his odd actions.

One friend of ours had a man who simply refused to take his shoes and socks off in bed. One day she just tore them off him in a fury. It turned out that he'd been tagged!

Dumping Survival – Drink Dialling

OK, so you're officially a member of the dumped club. Welcome on board. It's a bummer, isn't it? Don't worry. We know exactly what to do.

The good thing is that you're now in for a period of thorough self-indulgence. Personally, we wouldn't bother doing a stroke of work just now. If the boss starts having a go just burst into tears and say your heart is broken. Take a long sickie.

You're also are allowed extra calories too as sulking, managed properly, burns up extra energy. But more of that later. First of all –

before another word – you need to delete his number from your telephone. Delete it from your address book. Throw away your old phone statements that have a note of it from the twenty loving little texts you used to send every night.

All the good advice we're going to give you here will be simply ruined if you then go and get hammered and start ringing him. Dignity always, please. Even in defeat.

No drink dialling.

Really, sisters. We mean it. Phoning him when under the influence is the worst thing to do. Just imagine how stupid you'd have looked in the days before mobile phones. Can you really imagine your mother drunkenly turning up outside someone's window in the middle of the night and bleating their name over and over again. What do you mean, 'yes'? Give her this book immediately.

Just delete that number. You're not going to need it again now you've got us. Remember, you're a naughty girl. Naughty girls don't dial lost loves and beg for their return. They just get dialling someone far more fabulous.

The Naughty Girl's Guide to

SULKING OVER MEN

Now then. You *need* to sulk for a bit. Forget all that rubbish about going to the gym or finding mentally stimulating pastimes where you might meet new people. That's just patronising guff written by smug married psychologists who've forgotten what it's like to be dumped.

Remember, we started writing this book when we were in the same position as you. Life feels rotten – you're in no fit state for nonsense like Pilates. No, we say the best thing you can do is enjoy a period of major self-indulgent wallowing.

We'll go through exactly how to sulk and what to eat in a second, but first we want you to do a little maths. We're afraid there is a time limit to all this holed-up and bleary-eyed business.

The acceptable time allowance for sulking is ten per cent of the total relationship.

So, you went out for a year? OK, you can wallow in self-pity for a month, four days and about five hours.

If it was just a month, you need to pull yourself together in about three days.

If your one-night stand doesn't call then really don't let it bother you past elevenses. The only man-size thing you should be yearning for is a Mars bar.

Stick with this rule. Sharon once wallowed for years resulting in a butt so big she ended up on the same weight-loss show as Anne Diamond and Rik Waller.

Jennifer Aniston once said you can only be a victim for a day. Personally, we don't think we could have got over Brad Pitt that quickly. It's taken us a whole lot longer to get over some men who were a whole lot uglier. Maybe it's an American thing. Or perhaps we Brits are just much better at sulking.

Once the stiff man has gone, it's perfectly acceptable for the stiff upper lip to go too. Don't be a victim all your life, but now that your love life is out the window you're entitled to be one for just a little while. In fact, it's quite enjoyable.

Here's what to do.

How to Sulk With the Girls

One of the things you need to do within a week of getting dumped is to get absolutely blind-drunk. (See, told you we'd make it fun.) This should be done in public with your single mates. (NB: Do remember that if you've been in rehab then when we say wine, we mean chocolate cake for you.)

Do not invite anyone who's married or in a long-term relationship. They might well give you great advice and be great friends, but at the end of the night they're going to disappear off home for a hug with their understanding other halves to talk about how worried they are about you. You'll be left all depressed in the taxi as you go home alone and it will only make you feel worse.

No, the early stages of grieving should be strictly limited to your single friends who are also manless, hopeless and secretly wondering if they'll ever get laid again. That way you can all sit round together and wonder loudly why none of you can get a man as you're all so (delete as appropriate) witty/fabulous/generous/large breasted/rich/well dressed/thin.

Arm yourself for the night. Take along a selection of letters/voicemails/texts that he has sent you. Make sure you take the most loving ones so you can repeatedly say you do not understand how he can have changed his mind and so your friends can agree. Show the texts you sent him when you realised you'd been dumped. Again,

edit for effect and just show the ones that were fabulously witty or cutting. Don't, for goodness' sake, show the ones where you begged.

As you're liable to become completely sloshed/get into a cake-eating sugar frenzy, do check before you leave that his number is definitely deleted from your phone as we told you. Simply forward all his messages to your own number so you can safely show the girls without anyone drunkenly deciding they are going to ring him. Bear in mind that any good work from the night will be completely ruined by someone calling him to tell him how heartbroken you are.

CHECKLIST

❑ *It's compulsory to end the night concluding that all men are bastards. This is a wide-sweeping and unfair generalisation but it's appropriate for the occasion. Because let's face it, girlfriend – the only BJ in your life right now is Bridget Jones.*

❑ *You should also loudly discuss all of those friends of yours who are in relationships and decide that they're not really happy or well suited. It's good if your friends can try and bring along some examples to illustrate this – details of recent rows, news that people have put on weight or newspaper cuttings slagging them off.*

❑ *Wear your most fabulous outfit – the one that makes you look your hottest. This will ensure you arrive to a storm of compliments from the girls.*

  NB: If you're invited to a trashing-the-ex, girlfriend-boosting-evening like this, don't overdo it. Agree wholeheartedly with everything the dumpee says, but going over the top can be embarrassing when you discover a few days later that they have reunited with the ex. Save the really personal destruction until they are well past the recommended ten per cent sulking period and you should be safe.

❑ *If the ex at any stage tried to get lucky with you, we suggest you do not mention this either, until you're absolutely sure she hasn't thought about him for at least six months.*

❑ *If you let him get lucky, it is important to keep this very, very quiet.*

How to Sulk Alone

Yes, you need to do all the public wailing with the girls but you also need some private sulking time on your own as an essential part of the recovery process. If possible, we suggest making this *at least* a fifteen-hour session. It will help get everything out of your system.

Frankly, you're in no fit state for work and shouldn't even think twice about pulling a sickie at this stage. We'll tell you how on page 136. Only think about popping back into the office when you run out of friends to complain to and you feel like moaning to your colleagues instead.

For maximum use of your sulking time, plan an empty house day in which you will be left alone to *slump on the sofa, chain-smoke, eat bad things and watch every single daytime TV show* right up until *Judge Judy* in the afternoon. Once she's on, it's entirely permissible to open a bottle of wine. We'd let you do it earlier but it's best avoided in case the gas man/local MP/neighbours/a TV crew comes round. (Again, if you're on the wagon, congratulations and don't stray now. Get the profiteroles on standby.)

Spending hours lying on the sofa listlessly watching the television and stuffing your face is not a sad, defeatist way of dealing with rejection. Neither is getting pissed on your own. They are both just perfectly understandable knee-jerk reactions to the realisation that life is s*** right now. Any self-help book that tells you differently has almost certainly been written by a married person who's forgotten what it's like.

This isn't a permanent arrangement, of course, it's designed to move you on to the recovery stages. We're being indulgent with you. But it's temporary. (Pretty soon we're going to have you out and banging to your heart's content.)

Here's how to do it properly:

◆ Your dress code should be gravy-stained and crumpled velour/cashmere/sweatpants (depending on your budget). You're in no fit state to iron anything at the moment so don't risk it.

◆ Do not wear items of his clothing. In fact, if we catch you so much as sniffing them just to remember his scent, we'll be very, very disappointed in you. Give all his clothes to Oxfam. In fact, donate all his possessions to Oxfam.

Should he have carelessly abandoned a Breitling or Chanel J12 watch on your bedside table, do not think for one second of returning it. And no, girls, you are not requisitioning it either. Instead, think what a lovely, expensive watch like that could do for an entire African village: how many water wells could be bored in the desert, and how many kids could be put through school. Donate it to a charity shop immediately. (If he gives you any flak, tell him you thought he was something of a philanthropist who'd be prepared to dispense with things of great value for the benefit of mankind. Let's face it, he was quite content to dispense with your feelings without a second's thought!)

◆ Let yourself go. If you have to leave the house, for example to collect more fags, then don't dress, just throw a large coat over everything and wear, if necessary, a paper bag over your head.

◆ Eyebrows should remain unplucked. Hair unbrushed. Legs unwaxed. Undercarriages untrimmed. Spots attacked. For God's sake, this is not time for grooming. You're in crisis. We'll have you looking fabulous later, trust us. You're allowed at this stage to hit rock bottom in order to emerge phoenix-like from your ashen-skinned, hairy body when you are good and ready.

◆ Do not contact him or take his calls. The idea is to have a private guzzling and grizzling process, not to humiliate yourself by letting him know that you're actually doing it.

◆ You might want to dig out some old photos of yourself in which you look particularly fabulous. Ask yourself how on earth he could be mad enough to give up gorgeous you. Use airbrushed images if necessary. We do. Tara has an image of herself clad in nothing but gold leaf which she uses especially for this sort of thing.

◆ A hired DVD for the evening-part of the sulking is essential. It's also essential to select the right one. The last thing you need right now is to watch thin Hollywood starlets romping about with actors you fancy. Don't worry, we're looking after you and a fully vetted sulk-friendly list follows on page 276.

◆ Forget the government's recommended guidelines on drinking (for AA members, here's the equivalent in chocolate-eating). You're in turmoil. You need at least a bottle of wine (family-sized Dairy Milk) and, if you're still wide awake after that, some Night Nurse in a shot glass (Cadbury's Drinking Chocolate). Drinking alone is not sad. It's part of the grieving process. No drugs though, please. There's no need to get silly about all this.

◆ Stockpile food ready for your sulk. Easy-cook stuff only, mind you. You're in no state to be messing about with hot stoves or sharp knives. And don't even think of a salad. In times of grief, you need to keep your strength up. You need at least four times the normal food portion allowance. You'll burn off calories sulking.

◆ Again, we're being temporarily indulgent here. These food inhalation sessions are not permanent. One of the best things about breaking up is that you lose loads of weight and we'd hate to rob you of the opportunity of finally getting the flat stomach you've craved.

◆ Right then. You're all set. Now wallow. You can do all the 'playing sports and mingling with exciting new friends' bit later. At the moment, you've got to wallow in peace.

Sulking is the way forward.

CHECKLIST

❑ *A family-sized capriccioso pizza with extra cheese, double salami and extra olives is an acceptable light snack at this stage.*

❑ *Chocolate is good.*

❑ *Black Forest gateau is v good.*

❑ *With double cream is v v good.*

❑ *Large pots of caviar are even better.*

❑ *Do not watch any programmes featuring Gillian McKeith. We don't know anyone who eats mung beans in times of crisis.*

❑ *Fortune cookies rock (they always contain good news).*

How To Sulk In Public

Do plan your first venture into the outside world with care. Do not appear on *Trisha/Jeremy Kyle/Jerry Springer* begging for 'one last chance'.

And all the good you've just done with that self-indulgent wallowing will be completely undone unless you thoroughly plan all trips to make sure you stay away from couples. If you're facing life with a large 'reject' sign on your forehead, the last thing you need is to be surrounded by people looking like Ali MacGraw and Ryan O'Neal in *Love Story*.

So avoid the couple haunts. Don't go to the cinema, don't visit art galleries. Don't even think about going anywhere near Harrods Food Hall.

You're just not ready. We recommend staying away from bed shops too. Sharon once tried to cheer herself up post-break-up with some new high-threadcount linen. She went to a bed shop. A couple were trying out a mattress in Selfridges and were practically putting it to the ultimate test in the middle of the store. They were even spooning. After forlornly purchasing her kingsize sheets for one, she went home in a strop.

Turn down all invitations from sympathetic, happy-looking couples who try and fix you up at dinner parties. You just won't be in the mood – you'll end up as the single-one-out amongst the perfect pairs.

Tara's friends once tried to fix her up with a man who'd shelled out thirty million pounds to fly to the moon. His opening line was, 'It only took me seven seconds to get into orbit.' She replied, 'How long does it take to get into a packet of Wrigleys?' We still think that was quite funny. He didn't. The romance ended before it began and, needless to say, the earth did not move for the Moon man that night.

Most importantly – and this is a strict order – do not follow the well-meaning advice of friends who suggest you jet off to an exotic location to 'get over things'.

You will not come back looking tanned, fantastic and relaxed. You will spend the entire trip alone, watching people holding hands as they happily frolic in the surf together on their romantic break. Meanwhile, you'll sit alone and end up drinking your minibar dry. Actually, when Sharon did this she didn't even get to have a minibar. She totally forgot to look up when Ramadan started: that week in the honeymooners' resort in Dubai was a nightmare.

A singleton is the biggest threat going to any paired-up woman. Consequently, you will be totally shunned, eating alone as they steer their red-blooded unreliable men away from you.

Even worse, should any couples be generous enough to talk to you, you'll have to endure deadly dull descriptions of shopping trips, museums, sightseeing tours or stomach-churning accounts of last night's romantic dinner. The worst is when they insist on showing you the photographs of them laughing happily into the camera together. This can cause deep pain, particularly when you remember that the only holiday pickies you have are of you with a glass in your hand, photographed by one of the waiters.

Take it from us. Stay and sulk at home.

Apart from anything else, it's a lot cheaper.

STYLE TIPS
❏ *Do not pluck your eyebrows when you're pissed/distraught.*
❏ *Do not head for a new haircut and ask for something 'radically different'. You won't look like Halle Berry with even better cheekbones. You will hate it. Just because you're a mess, doesn't mean your hair should be as well.*

It is however
perfectly acceptable
to blow a fortune
on clothes. Rodeo Drive in LA is good if
you've still got access to his credit card.
Top Shop and Primark are perfectly
acceptable substitutes if not.

❑ *Having said that, a deep-conditioning treatment, an inch off the ends and a long scalp massage has been known to be beneficial.*

❑ *Do not risk spur-of-the-moment cosmetic surgery for the same reasons. He would still have dumped you even if you'd had a twenty-two-inch waist, a double-D cup and Angelina Jolie's lips. Beauty goes deeper than skin and we'll have you beautiful by the end of the book. (Yes, we know we're planning boob jobs, but that's different and we've really thought about it.)*

❑ *It is however perfectly acceptable to blow a fortune on clothes. Rodeo Drive in LA is good if you've still got access to his credit card. Top Shop and Primark are perfectly acceptable substitutes if not. After all, Spenderella, we're going to make sure we get you to the ball soon.*

Right then. This is pretty much the end of the wallowing bit. We've let you hit rock bottom for a while but if *we* can get through it all and still look this fabulous then so can you, sister. Now, go get yourself a manicure. We're going to take you by the hand and teach you how to be naughty.

The
Naughty
Girl's Guide to
REVENGE

(Any would-be bunny boilers are advised to please read through right to the *end of the chapter* before taking ANY action.)

The self-help books bang on about the elastic band theory for the man who won't commit. You know, all that stuff about letting them go and they'll come back to you.

Well, it's bloody obvious they're not going to come back now, isn't it? You've been dumped and dumped on a permanent basis and not just until his elastic band snaps back or he comes out of his man-cave, or whatever.

At times like this a girl's thoughts may naturally turn to revenge. For your information, here are some avenues that have been explored.

- There's the classic trick of sewing raw prawns into his curtains, sowing grass seeds in his shagpile or making him do a spot of sewing by cutting the arms off his suits.
- You could spend a lot of time advertising his work telephone number in rent-boy haunts with messages like 'wannabe ladyboy seeks to fund op'.
- Spycatchers in London sell bugging and recording devices so you could broadcast all sorts of interesting stuff over the loudspeakers of his office/local supermarket/pub.
- You could call the *News of the World* (020 7782 1000) and tell them about his darkest sexual habits. (NB: If he's a Premiership football player you should get at least ten thousand pounds if you do this. If it was Stan Collymore it's only really worth a few quid these days, though. There's been that many. Or ex-soapstars like Dean Gaffney. If you've just left Chris Tarrant's bed, then we're sorry but the *News of the World* can barely be bothered to pick up the phone these days.)

But that's all a bit cheap, isn't it? When people ask how you're getting on, it's much better they get the reply, 'Oh God, she's well over him, looks absolutely amazing and is in the throes of an all-consuming love affair with someone soooo much more exciting.' Do any of the above and you risk the reply, 'Her? Oh, she's a bunny-boiling madwoman. Wouldn't touch her with a bargepole after the way she behaved. You'd think she was the first person in the world to get dumped. We rarely see her these days, she's too busy doing community service.'

No, the best thing to do is to call the girls again. This time ask them to have a night in with you. The advantages of a night in are that you can get even more drunk as there are no bar staff to glare at you. Plus, you can slag off men even more vocally without other customers looking at you in pity.

Spend the evening with your most trusted girlfriends, drinking Chardonnay and discussing what you'd like to do to the little bastard. Ask for ideas. Write down their suggestions. Then go to bed with a large glass of water, some Rescue Remedy, Origins No Puffery™ eye mask and a dash of Chanel No.5.

In the morning, read the list. It will be the mad rant of drunken women. See how crazy it makes you look. See how illegal it all is. Don't do any of it.

Quite frankly, you've wasted enough time and energy on that loser. It's time to go on to the next stage of recovery.*

NB: If you ever do get back together it may be an idea to burn this list.

CHECKLIST
Do not

✗ *Boil any of his pets. (Not even if he owns a lobster farm and you're really hungry.) Boiling pets is bad. If you want to do that sort of thing we don't want you reading our book. Take it back and get a refund. Put the cash towards checking into a clinic.*

✗ *Even THINK about spraying on some of that aftershave he left in your bathroom. If you do go straight back to page 7 and read us properly this time.*

✗ *Stalk him in any way. He'll see your car even if you're parked right at the end of his street. He will not believe*

---

*Although, having said that, one girlfriend has just rung to say that, even in the cold sober light of day, the idea of writing insults on his lawn in weedkiller (see page 28) is so good that we just can't talk her out of it *that you just happen to be meeting someone in his local bar. He will not think it's a 'nice surprise' that you've just got a job with his firm.*

✓ *On the other hand, if you're likely to be his boss this could be quite funny and you should ignore our advice in this situation.*

Trust us. You won't win him back. You will just look undignified.

Do not do it.

The Naughty Girl's Mini Guide to Recovery

Now then, madam. That's quite enough wallowing and sulking, thank you! It was necessary but now it's getting boring. If you're still not over him by the end of your officially allowed sulking time then have a read through the following. Quite honestly, if you don't agree with at least one fact on the following list we don't think you're trying hard enough.

◆ There are six billion people in the world. One of them has got to fancy you.

◆ Everyone gets dumped. We have been. You have been. Even Jennifer Aniston has been. (If you haven't been then why are you reading this book, smug face?) It doesn't matter how beautiful, how rich, how wonderful you are. Life sometimes just happens that way.

◆ Anyway, we've heard that some of the most beautiful women in the world who are enjoying a very messy sex life are positively riddled with STDs. So the grass isn't always greener.

◆ Cheer up. At least you're not pregnant.

◆ And if you are, you can always nail him via the Child Support Agency.

◆ We bet you didn't actually feel that good when you were with him. Thinking the other person doesn't love you and fighting to try and make them is the loneliest and most soul-destroying feeling in the world. Didn't you just hate being on tenterhooks all the time?

◆ You do get over being dumped. Has it happened before? Now, if you're honest, do you really still wish you were with that creep? Really, honestly? Remember the guy who wouldn't play kiss-catch with you at primary school if necessary. Look him up on Friends Reunited. Bet he's a loser now.

◆ Just think about it. There were things he did that annoyed you. You had doubts, which you buried. Every girl goes into a relationship with rose-tinted spectacles and forgives his faults. We bet you bitched about him to your girlfriends sometimes. (Of course, any friend reminding you at this point that you said you wanted to marry him should be told to piss off. Their job is simply to agree with you and your current decision.)

Anyway. Never mind why he dumped you. What was wrong with HIM? Forget the positives. List the negatives.

Write that list here. Go on to a fresh piece of paper if necessary. Go on to several. The more the merrier, we say.

YOUR LIST

_____
_____
_____
_____
_____
_____
_____
_____
_____
_____
_____
_____
_____
_____
_____
_____
_____
_____
_____
_____
_____
_____
_____
_____
_____

Oh come on, don't stop now. The average ex has at least two pages worth of faults. Have you gone through all his bad bedroom habits yet? (We bet you can get a long list out of his shortcomings.)

_____

_____

_____

_____

_____

_____

_____

_____

_____

_____

_____

_____

_____

_____

_____

_____

_____

_____

_____

_____

_____

_____

Think hard. You must be able to come up with something. Did he wear horrible socks? Horrible SHORT socks? Horrible SHORT, SMELLY socks? Bad socks can easily be blamed for the malfunction of even the best relationship if you are prepared to try hard enough.

CLEARLY, HE'S AN IDIOT.

Otherwise why on earth didn't he realise how wonderful you are? Oh, look, we'll give you a few of our own.

SHARON: His habit of coming to bed in a pair of pyjamas marked 'World's Best Dad' was *such* a turn-off.

TARA: I got sick of him nicking my lipstick.

Remember this: you would have been shackled to him for the rest of your life. But one bedroom door closes and the next one opens. You've no idea who you might fall in love with next. Girlfriend, that's exciting.

You should be having a lot more fun.

It's time we told you how.

The Naughty Girl's
Guide to Being
SINGLE AND SEXY

Grant me the serenity to accept that sleeping alone
means I can apply moustache bleach whenever I like

Courage to get through the agony of an empty post
box on Valentine's Day

And the wisdom to realise those smug flowered-up types
secretly long to cuddle up alone with a good book, a
scented candle and a duvet that doesn't smell of
someone else's bottom.

There are girls out there who go from man to man. They trip gaily from fiancé to fiancé, haven't eaten a meal alone since primary school, have never been dumped, have never been lonely, and have never lain awake at night wondering if they'll ever get laid again.

This book is not written for them. In fact, if that sounds like you then please get your smug little nose out of our pages.

Has she gone? Good. Right, where were we?

Of course, by the time you reach the end of this book you'll be looking and feeling so fabulous, you'll be fighting off a hoard of rampant men. But in the meantime, here's how to be a singleton, live alone and *love* it.

You know what, not having a man gives you so much free time. You can get eight hours' sleep, do well at work and still get to the gym, the hairdresser's and go shopping. Be completely and utterly selfish because this is the one time in your life when you can. We want you to embrace being alone. Remember, solo is so chic. If you're going around thinking, 'poor me, I'm single', then go to the nearest mirror and give yourself an extremely stern glare before you read this chapter. Listen, you're not going to get lucky if you've got a long face and just hang around at home sulking and wearing bad knickers.

What do you mean, 'poor me'? You just happen to be between boyfriends. You have been blessed with delicious liberty, a lovely flat all to yourself, you're never locked out of the loo or faced with an empty loo roll. You are a fabulous and independent woman. You can go and flirt with anyone you want and not feel guilty.

Your bedsheets have a high threadcount, not a high fart count. You don't have to hide the Jolene. You do not have to fake an interest in football or grouse shooting. You have your own space. If you want to dance around in your knickers and Louboutin shoes at midnight you can. With the entire boxset of *Desperate Housewives* playing in the background.

You have a fabulous freedom and no one to stop you.

There are millions of women out there, squabbling with their boyfriends, picking his pants up off their floor, lying awake listening to screaming babies and wishing they were in your fabulous singleton high heels. Well, thousands if not millions.

If you smack of energy, excitement and happiness then people will want to be with you. In fact, men will start chatting you up. That's all because you've got an aura of fabulousness and confidence about you.

You may not feel that fabulous and confident right now, but here's how to fake it and look like you're getting it even when you're not.

The Workplace

One of the worst things about being single is that all the coupled-up people in the office think it's perfectly acceptable to talk in pitying, patronising tones about your sex life.

They all say smugly that 'it will come when you're not looking for it' and pat you on the back sympathetically as you go home alone each night.

The naughty girl needs to nip this sort of nonsense in the bud. Do all the crying you want at home but your image in the office should be of a woman with mystique, a wanton sex kitten being chased by dozens of men, who spends her days deciding who to choose and when.

Think Madonna in her slut days.

At least once a month you should come in carrying a bag from a good lingerie shop – like Agent Provocateur. If you can't afford to shop in these places simply borrow one of their carrier bags (see page 188). Make sure you walk past the desk of any attractive men in the office carrying the bag. It will earn you the reputation of a woman who invests in alluringly delicious smalls. Even if it's just holding the romantic girlie paperback that has become your dependable companion, it doesn't matter a scrap. They won't have a clue and your reputation should orbit.

(NB: If you decide to carry your sandwiches in the carrier bag then be careful not to go for egg or tuna. The aroma may carry and people will talk.)

Once in a while, try turning up at the office slightly late, hair unbrushed and wearing the same clothes as the day before. Make sure it's a showstopper of an outfit with stockings, seams and high heels that everyone will remember from twenty-four hours ago. They'll think you're a reckless adventuress leading a wildly exciting private life. For added effect use make-up to create dark rings under the eyes.

Even if the only person you had sex with last night was you, it'll still do your image the world of good.

Valentine's Day

We know, Valentine's Day is depressing. Sitting there with absolutely no deliveries, while all the other girls have half of Kew Gardens on their desks and can't even see their computers for all the blooms.

First, cheer yourself up by scanning the tabloids for details of break-ups or love rats to remind yourself that love can go wrong. If you can't find anything there just Google Darren Day or Brad Pitt. Then, distract yourself from everyone else's smug little love bliss bubbles by getting your own back and sending some flowers to yourself.

The one thing that makes smug flowered-up married types jealous is women who get to choose new lovers.

Arrange for these to arrive two weeks *after* Valentine's Day. This will look like your mystery lover sends you flowers at random just because they are maddeningly in love with ravishing you. An added advantage is that everyone else's Valentine's flowers will be dead by then.

Make sure that the message sounds secret and mysterious. Include a foreign phrase or American spelling to hint at an exotic overseas lover – perfect example: 'Red roses, your favorite color, remember?' or, 'Red roses for a perfect English rose, remember?' If no one picks up on it, you can point out that the sender can't even spell. Someone is bound to work it out eventually. Make sure it is a morning delivery to maximise on a whole day of speculation as you examine the message, saying, 'Oh my God, it isn't even Valentine's Day – who on earth could these be from, when did I wear red, and what did I say?' By 5 p.m. start strutting around with a secret smirky smile playing on your lips. This will convince all the busybodies in the entire office that you have identified the sender. As you sweep out, casually ask if LA is ten hours in front or behind.

This will create the illusion of you as a woman who is being chased by new bloom-bearing suitors. The one thing that makes smug flowered-up married types jealous is women who get to choose new lovers. Especially as, let's face it, most of them probably stopped doing it years ago.

CHECKLIST
- ❏ *Do not nip home early on Valentine's Day to nick flowers off the doorstep of any neighbours who have not arrived home in time to pick up their beautiful bouquets. (Unless they're very, very late in which case they're clearly not that bothered so you may as well have them.)*

❏ *Do take the behaviour of the smug couples gracefully. Don't make vomiting noises or wear a black armband or start crying. Do not 'accidentally' deadhead all the other people's bouquets when they go out to lunch. This is bad.*

❏ *It is also completely unacceptable to take flowers from hospital patients or graveyards. Even if you are in a really foul mood.*

❏ *Our TV gardener points out that a single drop of weed-killer in the vases will make sure the flowers last less than twenty-four hours. But only do it if they're being unbearable.*

It won't be long before your real-life fabulous lover emerges. But until that point you will go through some low points as a singleton. It is hard but remember you're not alone. At least you don't have pretend you like their cr*p gifts. Tara once made the mistake of telling a prince she liked the pancakes in Plaza Athénée in Paris. Two were hand delivered every day for the next three months until she eventually emigrated in despair.

Christmas

Christmas can be depressing. It's the time of year when relatives and parents just can't help themselves commenting about your love life. Going home for Christmas, staying in your childhood bed and being told about how everyone in your school year has now given birth except you can be tough. All you've got is your granny saying how 'you've grown'. And you can't help wishing you had a man to say that to on Christmas Day.

Girls, you may feel like the only singleton in the village but the trick with Christmas is realising that you are not alone.

Across the world there are millions of singletons who spend Christmas Day being asked, 'Have you got a boyfriend yet?' There is no way of avoiding this, we're afraid. It's one of those family rituals that you just have to go through. In fact, the average girl will spend at least three decades being asked this question and answering 'no'. Chin up. We've been there, still doing that. Why do you think we're writing this book?

Christmas cards are another issue. Anyone who's in a relationship just can't help smugly signing their Christmas card from 'us' – rubbing it in for any lonely singleton who's still only signing the one name. Some ultra-smug couples have even been known to send cards with cheesy pictures of themselves in his-and-hers jumpers with little mini ones from their children or pets. Cheer yourself up by drawing comedy moustaches on them all or hold a competition for whose was the worst.

All Your Friends Are Giving Birth

Yes, yes, the joy of bringing new life into the world has eluded you thus far. But look on the bright side. The only stitching you have to worry about is how to afford that exquisite handstitched, rhinestone-encrusted Galliano. You will not be suffering cracked nipples, neither will you be leaking breast milk down the aisles in Sainsbury's.

Your flat stomach does not resemble an Ordnance Survey map.

Your perineum has not become a mausoleum.

Hoik your sag-free bosoms into a Wonderbra and go out and celebrate. Celebrate the fact that even if men aren't on your side, gravity is.

Sexual Frustration

Sorry, you'll just have to buy the sequel – *The Very Very Naughty Girl's Guide to Life*.

Across the world there are millions of singletons who spend Christmas Day being asked, 'Have you got a boyfriend yet?' Chin up. We've been there, still doing that. Why do you think we're writing this book?

Are you letting yourself go?

One of the disadvantages of being a singleton is that there's no one around to nag you to pull your stockings up if you're letting standards slip. That's where we come in. *We want you to take care of yourself*. If any of the following sounds familiar then we're sorry to tell you but you're turning into a sad old spinster and should stop immediately.

EATING
Are you mainly dialling for your dinner? Now, we're not going to start insisting you go all organic or vegan or anything but it is good to cook occasionally, you know. If more than two meals a week are arriving in a cardboard box on the back of a motorbike then we're going to get really cross with you. This rule applies even if you do fancy the delivery boy.

It's also inexcusable to go out and buy all those microwave meals for one. Make a quick tour of the supermarket until you reach the display featuring brightly coloured items, some with stalks. These are called fruit. The ones with leaves are called vegetables. Ask a member of staff for assistance if you are not too sure. These items are good for you. Greengrocers stock them too and will also give advice if required.

KNICKERS
We're going to take a guess here. Are your knickers grey? Are they big? Has the elastic gone? Go on, have a look. Have they passed their sell-by date? Are they older than the pizza delivery boy? If so, take them off. Immediately. (NB: Not if you're reading this on the tube.)

Remember: vintage goes in a glass. Not on your ass.

If your underwear is bad, then you will feel bad. Even if it's only you that sees them, we want you in pristine gussets all the time, please. Think of your pants as a Beaujolais Nouveau and go for a new range each year. New knicker elastic always pulls you in, perks you up and leaves you feeling fabulous.

In fact, we absolutely demand that you don't read another word until your bottom is encased in something beautiful. If we meet you in the street we may hold spot checks on this so please always remember.

BUYING A CAT
Cats are darned useful. But use them carefully.

Do

✓ *Copy your cat's walk. See how sexily it sashays around the flat, prettily swishing its tail, and practise doing the same. Strangers come and stroke your cat and it either coolly submits and allows them or rejects them and stalks off. Be that cat. Try and follow its fabulous example. Remember, cats never give a darn.*

✓ *Take full advantage of your position as a cat owner. If you want to check out the neighbours, you could pretend your cat has run off. Put on high heels and full make-up, then apply a little Carmex under the eye (see page 86) so you can cry prettily as you knock on their door and ask if they happen to have seen your lost cat. (We must point out that Carmex is designed to go on the lips but everybody in TV and movies uses this technique. And when we say under the eye we mean under and not in it). This technique allows*

you have a good look round their home and assess the
possibility of single males (wealthy and/or worth
revisiting). You can tell any potential candidate where you
live and give them your telephone number. There is even an
excuse to go back and visit them to say you've recovered the
cat safe and sound. Of course, when trying this trick
without owning a cat, do remember to at least buy a litter
tray and have some Whiskas lying about should the local
hunk come round to comfort you over your missing pussy.

Don't

✗ Become one of those bores whose dog/cat/budgie is their
child substitute, who has its photo on their screensaver
and rambles on and on in a baby voice about Piddles,
Tiddles or Biggles respectively. We've known cases of girls
actually holding birthday parties for these creatures and
insisting their parents send cards to their 'furry
grandchildren'. You may as well wear sixty denier.
Remember, we want you to look like a wanton sex kitten
who might invite a man back for a night of unbridled
passion, not a raddled old cat woman who'll make them
sit and watch you snogging Tiddles and boiling sardines.
We also ask that you only ever show off photographs of
your dog/cat/budgie in the first twenty-four hours after
purchase, please.

✗ Ring home and ask family or neighbours to put your pet
'on the phone'. It's not cute. It is unbearably sad.

✗ When we say 'copy your cat', don't overdo it. Don't, for
example, go jumping off walls. Don't grow whiskers. Avoid
fish breath. Don't screech outside people's windows in the
middle of the night. Stick to the sweet and sexily aloof bit.

HOUSEWORK

Put down this book and look at the floor for a second. Can you see your carpet? We hate to sound like your mother, but the one thing that is

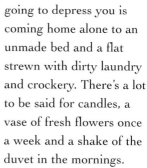

going to depress you is coming home alone to an unmade bed and a flat strewn with dirty laundry and crockery. There's a lot to be said for candles, a vase of fresh flowers once a week and a shake of the duvet in the mornings.

Before you leave the house each day, ask yourself if you would dare bring a new lover back here. You should never leave the place looking like the home of a complete slut unless you know for certain that your cleaner is coming that afternoon to hide the evidence.

DRINKING

All the self-help books say you should never
drink alone. It's the start of a slippery slope to
alcoholism, apparently. One glass of wine in front of
Coronation Street tonight and, before you know it, you'll
be a sad old alcoholic, pouring vodka on your
cornflakes with your life in ruins. This is, of course, tosh.

Just because you're single it doesn't mean you have to
sit there crying into your Evian, wishing you had a
boyfriend. Pour yourself a glass and enjoy it. Then have
another one. (If you're in recovery then well done and stay on
the wagon.)

There are some emergency circumstances (see page 41) in
which it is entirely acceptable to get hammered on your
own and follow all that with a slug of Benylin
just to help you sleep. But we don't want it
to become an everyday thing for you.
Drinking on your own is not a crime
but aim for pleasantly tipsy rather
than wrecked.

To slow it all down a bit, we recommend you run
a nice bath and get a book before finally sipping your
drink slowly in the warm bubbles. Necking neat gin out
of the fridge the second you get in is not a good look.

Drink like a lady. Don't throw back beer like a truck driver.

Actually, we nicked that advice off Kimberly Stewart,
who was given it by her dad Rod. Rodders is quite
right. Be a little less HGV-like in your drinking.

To help you judge your drinking, here are some frequent situations which occur after solo alcohol sessions and a guide to how often we'll allow it to happen before we get all disappointed in you and insist on an alcohol-free night.

DRINKING ALONE CHECKLIST

Falling asleep on the sofa mid-movie and mid-drink – Hey, don't worry. It could just be that you make really bad movie choices. If it's no more than once a fortnight we won't come round and nag you.

Leaving your make-up on and crawling into bed – Twice in a lifetime. Have some standards, woman. Just because you're always breaking up, don't start breaking out too. Cleanse and tone always, sister.

Having strange items arrive from eBay or late night TV shopping channels – Large glass was it? Once every two months is probably allowable unless you're buying things like Ferraris. Sharon once bought a painting of an elephant with a light-up moving trunk after a particularly splendid bottle of Merlot. One good trick is that when the shopping channel rings back to confirm the delivery in the morning, you simply say it was the 'kids, messing about on the telephone' and they should waive the purchase. Mind you, the elephant does look quite nice in the loo.

Men turning up from Internet dating agencies that you don't remember emailing – If you need to check your outbox for messages perhaps you need to check in. Even when it's just a modem, never drink and dial where men are concerned. Know your limits.

Phoning ex-lovers after midnight – No, no, no. Look, we thought we told you to delete his number (see page 33). Don't do it. Please don't tell us you left a voice message when he didn't pick up. He'll only play it to everyone to show them what a mad drunken old ex you are. If you really have an alcohol-fuelled urge to get in contact then send a text message that makes it look as if you've sent it by mistake. Something like, 'Please can we make the filming an hour later as I've only just got home?' Then if he texts back asking how you are and what you're filming so late at night, you might get away with it. But really, even that looks a bit suspect. The best thing to do is think of yourself as an enchanted pumpkin. Remember Cinderella? Nobody wants to know you after midnight.

Drunkenly attempting hardcore home bikini-waxing – You'll only do this once. Trust us. It may not hurt at the time but the results will be really bad.

CHECKLIST

✗ *Don't make the bottle your lover. We do allow you a drink but don't overdo it. Can you get through a night without it? Do you spend as much time with your bottle as you would with a man? If you're calling in sick because of hangovers, cancelling things or panicking if the Frascati's not in the fridge, then we're sorry. It's too much.*

Being a sexy single naughty girl is the most fun you'll ever have. But only if you get out there and enjoy it. If you go out less often than the Olympic Flame then you haven't made the most of it.

Unless the pizza delivery guy really rocks you'll never find Mr Right sitting on the sofa at home. Even if your flat is a lovely, peaceful, shiny and fluffy pussycat-filled heaven we want you out of it sometimes. At least twice a week. In high heels and (gusset-free) hosiery, please.

Don't let the world be deprived of fabulous you.

The Naughty Girl's Mini Guide to Self Help Books

Having said all that, if you want a man we'll help you. There's a whole host of advice out there from the Smug Marrieds. Some of it's good. Some sucks.

1) *Not Tonight, Mr Right* by Kate Taylor.

Advice: Refuse to have sex with your man for six months after you start dating.

Smug? Oh yes. She says she's met the man she's in love with. She held out. He loves her. They're married and everything's rosy. (She does admit she had a dreadful time before so at least she used to be one of us.) 6/10.

Suggestion: She says don't get horizontal until you're sure. Girls in their late twenties or early thirties are told they should ideally wait for an engagement ring. She reckons if you follow her advice and wait at least six months you could be married within the year.

Our advice: Six months? Oh my God. This isn't *Jane Eyre*. Do you really want a man who won't respect you unless you keep your knickers on until after you've both met the vicar and booked the church? Listen, if you only lasted six dates don't give yourself a complex. You're perfectly normal and won't look like a slut. If they give you diamonds you can get in there even sooner. They give you a rock, you get that bed a rockin'.

Kate will no doubt be very cross with this advice but rumour has it she did let her hubby-to-be get past first base by date twelve. Strumpet.

2) *Single to Settled* by Elizabeth Clark

Advice: Every day is an opportunity. Do a daily action plan and she guarantees you'll pull.

Smug? Very. She dedicates the book to her children, and to her ever so adoring hubby. Says she just couldn't have done the book without them. 8/10.

Suggestion: Stalk men in supermarkets, sidle up to them as they take something from the shelves. Then take a quick peer into his trolley, and comment about the most 'unusual' thing in there.

Our advice: Supermarkets are good because they're always packed with people. But this is a lousy pick-up line. And if all he's bought is some Preparation H, it could go horribly wrong.

We think you're much better off going to a bar, where the lighting is so much more flattering and there's alcohol. But one trick that does work in supermarkets is taking along an old mobile handset. Find someone you fancy then simply let your phone go smashing to the floor so the card and battery go bouncing all over the place.

It's the perfect excuse to let him help to retrieve the pieces. If things seem to be going well, point out that your phone is broken and casually ask to borrow his. Dial home, leave a fake message, then hand the phone back with a wink telling him that he's now got your home number if he'd ever like to call.

On a style note, if you're planning to pull in supermarkets then bear in mind there's bright lighting there: you'll need foundation and a bit of lippy so you don't look washed out. And the lighting is

even worse round the frozen
food section so avoid that.

Don't hang around the
condom section – it's way too
obvious.

Oh, and do pick your
supermarket with care.
Choose Fortnum and Mason
if you like your exotic
overseas lovers, Marks &
Spencers for city boys and, if
you're after a bit of rough,
try Iceland's frozen-turkey
counter. If they're at
Selfridges buying fabulous
skincare, we hate to break it
to you but he's gay.

3) *Superflirt* by Tracey Cox

Advice: Promises techniques to transform you into an instant and
fabulous seductress.
Smug? Not unbearably. But she can't resist pointing out that she's
happily 'settled'. 5/10.
Suggestion: Says to suck the end of your sunglasses, or start
caressing the stem of your wine glass in public. Apparently this is a
subtle way of suggesting what you might like to get up to later
with the lucky man you've got in your sights.
Our advice: This is a little too obvious. Pleasuring a wine glass on your
own? It's a little eighties. You're not in a Flake advert, you know.

A much better trick is to always pack twenty quid's worth of euros in your purse. You can then just lean over to the man as the drinks bill comes and ask if he knows if the bar takes euros or if he travels at all and is able to change it for you. He might tell you to sod off but it also gives him the perfect opportunity to buy you the drink. And you'll look all cosmopolitan and well travelled.

4) *He's Just Not That Into You* by Greg Behrendt and Liz Tuccillo

Advice: Greg says that if a bloke's messing you around, don't bother analysing it, just realise he's not that into you and move on quickly.
Smug? Greg does mention that he lives with his wife and daughter. But keeps it low key. 5/10.
Suggestion: (To cope with a man who's dumped you without bothering to tell you.) Says that you do not call them and shout at them. Greg says the man will only feel smug that he's had that big an effect on you and suggests you let someone else deal with him. He reckons you should just shut up and leave it. You're far too busy anyway. Getting on with all the other fabulous things that you have to do.
Our advice: OK, OK, it's probably the right grown-up advice but darn what *he* feels. Actually, sometimes we haven't got better things to do with our time. He's been cruel – why should you be cool? Once it's obvious he's disappeared on you (see page 19 for techniques of finding out) you should ring him repeatedly from a withheld number until he picks up. Threaten to chop his bits off if you like. You'll feel better for it, it's fun and it burns off calories. So what if you regret it? He's not coming back anyway. Besides, you're doing it for the sisterhood. He may just think twice about doing it to the next girl.

5) *The Rules* by Ellen Fein and Sherrie Schneider

Advice: Men want a challenge. Play hard to get.

Smug? Unbearably. They go on about their 'wonderful' husbands in the dedication. (Bleughh.) 8/10.

Suggestions: Never talk to a guy first otherwise you won't know if he's just responding out of forced politeness. You should never ask a man to dance either. Even if you're having a really boring, lonely evening on your own. And never stand next to someone you fancy hoping it'll help them notice you. The man has to do all the running or he won't think you're worth it. And if you ever feel like breaking The Rules you should go home and do sit-ups instead.

Our advice: Sod that. It's *never* better to go home and do sit-ups.

This might work in America where everybody does this multiple dating thing and they're all off for dinner with each other every three minutes. But it doesn't work in Britain where the men are shy. Sharon tried it once and ended up watching forlornly in the corner on her own as Alicia Douvall raced around the room collecting phone numbers. We say it's best to march up to one of the little schmucks and grab him. So what if it all goes wrong? The worst that can happen is that you get turned down for a dance. Carpe diem. Seize the day. Seize the bloke. If he tells you to back off, then there's still time to go home and do sit-ups on your own.

Although having said that, credit where credit's due, we do love the bit in *The Rules* where they tell you how to treat a guy on the phone. It says you should never call a man, always let them call you. Never accept a date for a Saturday unless he's asked you by the Wednesday. And always put the phone down first saying (nicely) that you're really busy and have to go. Trust us. This 'being elusive' stuff really works. Thanks for that. You couple of Smug Marrieds, you.

Carpe diem.
Seize the day.
Seize the
bloke

6) *The Man Manual* by Linda Papadopoulos

Advice: Reckons she knows absolutely everything you'll ever need to know about your man. *Smug?* Points out that she has a husband and daughter. 5/10. *Suggestions*: Psyche yourself up imagining you are a 'Bardot-esque sexpot' who absolutely everyone in the office has the hots for. Then wait until the end of the day, approach the man you've got your eye on as he's packing up his desk. And simply saunter past casually and ask if he's up for a quick drink.

Our advice: 'OK. This probably works if you are actually a Bardot-esque sexpot. Which, having met her, this authoress is. But for the rest of us, this advice just doesn't work. You have to be much, much cleverer about asking out colleagues. If it all goes wrong then everyone finds out about it, and this casual stroll thing just won't look casual.

A much better idea is to do a group email, which he's cc'ed in on, asking if anyone fancies a drink later. If he likes you, he'll be there. OK, you may end up stuck with just the dull bloke from Accounts but you can always cut your losses after one G&T. Even better, go and invest a bit. Find out who he supports and get two tickets, or buy tickets for a great gig. Then do a round robin email saying someone's just dropped out and ask if anyone fancies coming along with you.

Make the email company-wide and include a couple of email addresses of people from outside the office. Sit back. If he emails back then of course you ignore all the other replies and tell him his came first. If he doesn't reply then we're sorry, he's just not interested in you. If the only bloke who replies is that bloke from Accounts again then simply tell him you're sorry but a male friend from outside the office replied first.*

OK, it takes a bit of investment to get the hot tickets. But sometimes you've got to spend money to save face. You can always take a girlfriend along instead or flog the tickets on eBay.

---

* Then again, you know this bloke from Accounts is clearly into you. Is he really a loser? He could be very handy if it's tax return time.

7) *Why Mr Right Can't Find You . . . And How to Make Sure He Does* by J.M. Kearns

Advice: That you don't need to lose weight, or learn about football. Just find out where all the single available perfect men hang out. And go there.

Smug? Yes. Mentions his partner who's called Debra. And their little pussycat. Who's called Murphy. 6/10.

Suggestions: Actually really rather good. He says to try bars, try work, try parties, try bookshops and smile at men that you like to give them encouragement. There's also a particularly brilliant anecdote about a girl who landed herself with lots of dates after finding a job in the Debenham's Men's Clothing Department.

Our advice: Now this menswear thing is excellent advice. Tara once worked for a tailor in Savile Row and spent her whole day, with her tape measure, nose to crotch. Measuring inside legs was the fastest track to securing dates. Come to think of it – she can't remember why on earth she left.

8) *How To Make Anyone Fall in Love With You: 85 Proven Techniques for Success* by Leil Lowndes

Advice: Reckons she's got the quick way of achieving success in love.

Smug? She calls herself Ms Lowndes and makes no boasts of a significant other. 1/10. We presume she must have one though because, looking at Amazon, she's written stacks of books on love.

Suggestions: Actually quite comprehensive, listing fifty-three studies as part of her research and giving strict instructions on eye contact, smiling and compliments. Then she goes and ruins it all by suggesting girls rent out a porn movie to pick up some 'raw sex' techniques.

Our advice: Look, men are just grateful when you take your clothes off. If you want technique then take a cucumber round to your gay friends and ask for helpful tips. But men's porn films are not a good way to see love. Tara was once approached by an mega international movie star who asked if she'd mind acting out one scene he'd seen in one. But as she told him, three is always a crowd. Especially on a first date.

9) *Humped Me, Dumped Me* by Yasmin Brooks and Cathy Gray

Advice: Says it will cheer you up, when he's scarpered after doing the deed.
Smug? Cathy is. Goes on about how she's all settled with 'The One'. 6/10.
Suggestions: All good stuff. They also hate drink dialling and say the best thing post-break-up is a bit of shopping. A bit too nice though. For example, they say that if he dumps you the day after you've given him his birthday present, you should be calm and philosophical about it. Says you should just sit quietly and take heart from the fact that he's another year older, that the grey hairs and middle-aged spread are on their way and that no one will want him when he's old.
Our advice: Oh, it's all so dignified. Look, if you think things are on the slide, always buy him things to wear so when he puts them on he'll think of you and remember what a heel he was. And personally, if the little git waited till he got his pressie to dump you, then you're perfectly entitled to use the 'weedkiller on the lawn' technique. Just make it personal. Write "F*** you, birthday boy'.

The Naughty Girl's Guide to DATING

Are you ready for a new man? Sometimes it can be a way to get over getting dumped. Do have a think and work out if this is best for you, though. You should never try and replace someone or fill the void with someone else.

Rebound rarely rocks and – trust us – you don't actually NEED a man in your life.

Ignore all previous dating advice you've been given. We know all those books suggest you find a new hobby like sculpting or Internet dating. But some of the advice being given out these days is really lousy. We read one book which suggested you should sidle up to men buying TV dinners at the supermarket and say, 'Is it a convenience thing? If not, the local restaurant is running cookery classes for busy professionals.'

Personally, we think that would make you look sad. You should stay clear of losers buying TV dinners for one. And stay clear of evening classes. Why the hell should you be condemned to spending your evenings making clay pots or weaving baskets just because you can't get a man?

Don't go down the newspaper/Internet ad route either. Could you honestly hold your head up and admit you met your partner by responding to an ad containing the acronyms WLTM or GSOH?

If you really want to go out and trap strangers in public, then do what Tara does. Go to The Ivy and ask the waiters if they'd take a note round to the table of any guy that takes your fancy. Shock tactics can bring surprising results. Otherwise, here are some tips our girlfriends gave us. We don't think they're illegal. So why not give them a go?

Hitch-hiking by private jet

This has been known to work. But you'll need confidence and, if possible, couture to carry it off. You may also need a lawyer if you fail to explain what you're doing on a plane without a ticket.

Dress immaculately, go to the airport and then ask for the private jet area. Should anyone ask what you're doing wandering around, do not react as if it's a perfectly reasonable question. Instead, reply haughtily that you're waiting for someone.

Then find the ladies'. Get some Carmex lip balm and dot it under your eyes. This makes your eyes water. But prettily. Not in a way that leaves you with a streaming nose and a bright-red face. If you can't magic up some real tears then Carmex works wonders. (Obviously don't go over the top. You only need a dot under each eye. You're aiming for a solitary tear, not a waterfall.) Sit on a bench looking forlorn, yet f***able. And just wait for some rich man to come along. With a jet. Tara once hitched a lift in Quincy Jones's Gulf Stream using this exact method.

Take a bag, a passport and a clean pair of knickers.

If they try to arrest you, show them this book and explain you're under a great deal of mental strain and not thinking straight, or that you're doing research for the sequel. We recommend Heathrow Private Side, Farnborough Air Field and RAF Northolt.

Copping Off in a Bar

If you're scared of flying, try this. Decide which pop star/footballer/ playboy/polo team you fancy the most and work out which hotel they stay in when in town. Start by going to that hotel's cocktail bar. Go there a lot. Always look amazing. Tip the bar staff heavily so you get info on forthcoming parties, get given a rapturous welcome on arrival and are introduced to people.

We know one girl whose very rich husband had just left her for a younger woman and she just simply sat in the bar of a very chic hotel until her next rich husband came along. It took about a week. So this trick does work.

Again, this requires supreme confidence. And a decent wardrobe to avoid being mistaken for a local hooker. You could also use the Carmex for the forlorn but f***able look. Don't overdo it. You're after a sweet solitary tear. Not a streaming panda impression. Take appropriate reading material. *The Economist* if you want a City man, *Horse and Hound* if you prefer the country type, the *Spectator* if you must have an up-to-the minute cutting-edge sharp wit. Something with lots of nice pictures and not too much writing if you want a pop star. Interior decorating magazines if you don't mind your movie star husband being in the closet. Try to avoid wedding magazines. It'll only put them off.

And avoid the Ritz for tea, it's full of middle-aged tourists.

Oh, and don't risk a drink. Drink fruit cocktails until 9 p.m. or someone buys you a drink. If it doesn't work, at least you'll have stocked up on vitamins and your skin will be amazing.

Exercise

Don't bother with yoga or ballet. What's the point of torturing yourself if all you do is meet lots of women who are thinner and bendier than you? No, you may as well go and train with a rugby team. It may hurt but the view will be much more enjoyable.

Most training seasons start at the end of summer. Look them up on the Internet and find a team that does mixed-sex pre-season training sessions and sign up. Play your cards right and you should only have to do around two training sessions running round a field, charging into people or catching rugby balls before you've made enough male friends to be invited to after-training drinks. It'll also give you a chance to case the talent in their shorts.

After that you can just skip the training bit altogether and arrive, immaculately made-up and looking gorgeous, at the bar just as they all emerge sweatily from the pitch.

Remember, there are fifteen players in a rugby team. The odds are good.

And if you're really crap at sport there's always darts. The men may not be as fit or chunky, but there's always a bar.

Weddings

Weddings are renowned for matchmaking. There's plenty of champagne and everyone's in a good mood so here's your chance. The only people off-limits are the groom, the vicar and the pageboys. Other than that you've got carte blanche.

The father of the bride is fine. Although probably best not to make it more than a one-night stand. He'll be flat broke after spending all that money on his daughter's wedding anyway.

Funerals

Not really good form. Yes, we know you look thin and sexy in black. But we wouldn't go any further than a respectful exchange of cards at the wake. Especially if you were married to the deceased. Maybe best to let the body go cold first, hey?

CHECKLIST

✓ *You know, there are all these rules you're supposed to follow. Pretend to be busy. Pretend you don't care. Don't drink on the first date. Don't get your knickers off before you're engaged. It's true that a bit of mystique and a hard-to-get aura goes a long way. After all, most men are predators.*

✗ *But don't get so caught up playing the game that you don't enjoy it as well. Just get out and talk to people. Accept every party invitation. Say yes to going out with the girls. Have fun. Try different things. Don't make every occasion a desperate search for a soulmate. Just embrace life. And if you find a fab fellow along the way, then happy days. Smile at him. Seize him.*

✓ *Lie back and think, England. No, not of England, think of us – and thank us for all our fabulous advice.*

✓ *And don't worry if it doesn't work out. Just move on to the next. Remember, you'll never find Mr Right without going out and risking a few Mr Wrongs.*

The Naughty Girl's Mini Guide to Getting Naked

For style tips on what to wear for That Date, and how to undress without him realising you're wearing chicken fillets in your bra, see page 124. But right now we know that the biggest fear about being with someone new is that they won't like you with your clothes off. This is, of course, nonsense. Trust us. Any man will be delighted that you are naked.

Here to help you is our Rule of Thumb. Read it. Then go and get your kit off with confidence.

The Rule of Thumb

What does your thumb look like? Go on, think. You just think of it as a thumb-shaped thing, right? Have a look at it. It's probably not perfectly straight. The nail may not be perfectly groomed. It may be lined. A bit short. A bit fat. A bit rough in places. But when you look at it you never see any of that. You just see your thumb.

Now then, when you stand naked in front of a man you think he's seeing your lumpy bits, your fat bits, short bits, lined bits, rough bits. He's not. He is thinking, 'There is a naked woman in front of me.' He is thinking, 'Hurrah!'

He may also be thinking, 'Why is she reading that book right now?', which is why we recommend reading this chapter in advance.

We've taken you to the bedroom door. We've got you naked. We've shown you the rule of thumb. Now it's up to you. We've got you this far and we're sure you can cope perfectly well on your own from here.

If it all goes badly please turn back to page 83.

If it all goes well, we'll meet you on page 95 for some post-coital advice on how to avoid becoming a smug couple.

> CHECKLIST – THE NEXT MORNING
> ✓ *If at his, you will look really adorable wearing his men's pyjamas. Ask if you can borrow them. The added advantage is that if you've been desperately holding in your stomach all night then you can stop once you get these over-sized pjs on.*

✓ *If at yours, negligees from Myla are perfectly acceptable.
As are little silky sets from La Perla. Think skimpy. But
don't ever wear a thong. Nobody looks good in a thong.
The only possible exceptions are Brazilian carnival
queens but you need the full accessories, including
headdress and carnival band and cheering entourage, to
carry it off. These can be impractical on a first date.*

✗ *Don't polar bear it in a towelling robe, either. Get off
your iceberg, sister. You're there to be his hot lover.*

The Naughty Girl's Mini Guide to Being a Bit of a Tart. And Getting Away With it.

Of course, the problem is that as you turn into a fully fledged
wanton sex kitten and naughty girl – you also turn into a bit of a
tart. At some point you'll hear those six little words every woman
dreads from her man, 'How many lovers have you had?'

Personally, we've been through quite a few. Tara claims half of
Sharon's iPod.

Do not, when asked, grab a calculator and work them all out in
front of him. That's such a bad look. Especially if you start writing
them all down and have to ask for another sheet of paper. The best
thing to do is remember that some lovers were just not your fault.
So there's no point in counting them.

Have a quick flick through our checklist and if the following occurred during any of your love affairs then there's no need to declare them at Lover Customs.

CHECKLIST

❏ *He looked like Quasimodo. You can disallow all ugly lovers. If you'd be too embarrassed to show a photograph of them, then there's no need to admit you slept with them.*

❏ *Holiday Romances. Again, no need to declare. If none of your work colleagues or friends met them, then officially they didn't exist. So it's OK, girlfriend, you go and cross all those little surfer boys off the list. (Do be careful that they won't turn up though – see page 219 for tips on how to avoid this.)*

❏ *Those whose surnames you don't recall. Those whose any-names you don't recall. If the love affair didn't last long enough for you to start practising your new married signature then don't worry about it.*

❏ *One-night stands. It would be entirely human to sheepishly admit to having had one of these. But say that it didn't feel good, so you never did it again. Don't ever admit to having tried it more than once. If the relationship was over by breakfast it wasn't worth mentioning. (If you didn't even make it to the full one-night stand and just did the 'stand' bit with someone, then that is a bit sluttish and it's probably best not to mention that.)*

❏ *If they dumped you, rule them out. It doesn't matter if you were married to them for ten years. They left, so technically they wouldn't have been an ex if you'd had your way. So there's no need to declare them.*

❏ *Celebrities don't count. It would be terribly indiscreet to gossip about them and you don't want to look like one of*

> *those kiss-and-tell girls. And you'll only end up looking cheap if your chosen celeb then goes on to have some sort of sex scandal. Of course if he was an A-list Hollywood lead it might be worth a mention. But if it was just a guy from EastEnders, we really wouldn't bother.*

> ❏ *Those that you didn't inform your parents about. If they never met, or were never mentioned to their future in-laws then, really, they couldn't have been that important. So they don't exist.*

And by now we should be bringing you down to a something-like-respectable figure. So it's basically only long-term relationships, where they had met your parents before you dumped them. With luck this should bring you down to about one or two.

OK, you shouldn't push it and wear snow-white on your wedding day, you little harlot, but look how many other whites they list on the Dulux paint chart.

If, after all this you're still pushing into double figures then really you should lie through your teeth. In your teens only admit to one other lover. By your twenties it's OK to have three notches on the bedpost. After that we really wouldn't ever declare higher than seven.

Don't ever go into double figures.

CHECKLIST

❏ *If you're pretending to be a virgin and claim it's your first time, try and remember to say 'ouch'. And then cry afterwards.*

The Naughty
Girl's Guide to being
A SMUG COUPLE

Grant me the serenity to recognise that just because
I'm getting it regularly there's no need to be so smug

Courage to occasionally prise myself away from my lover
and check the girls are OK

And the wisdom to realise that there's a chance this man
may not be for life – but the girls definitely are and
they need me too.

If you've just hooked up and you're reading this chapter, then congratulations. You're a true member of the sisterhood and a good friend who realises that just because you've now got a man it's worth discovering how not to rub everyone else's sad single faces in it.

If you just happened to have found this book on the bathroom floor, casually opened at this page, then we suggest you read on and don't stop reading until you reach page 117. Especially if this paragraph's been highlighted. Sister, we hate to say it but you've turned into a Smug Couple, and somebody's trying to tell you something. You're so caught up in your little bubble of bliss that

you're seriously doing everyone's head in. It's not that we don't love you any more, it's just that you need a gentle hint. It may be great for you, but it's starting to grate on the girls.

Don't worry, there is a way forward. There are just a few little rules we'd like you to follow to stop you turning into one of those women who everyone bitches about behind their back.

The Maths

First up, well done on finding a boyfriend. For a while back there in the desert you may have resigned yourself to life on the shelf as a sad lonely old hag like the rest of us. So, although we're a tiny bit jealous, we're also genuinely pleased that you've found someone fabulous in your life and are now getting it regularly.

We do understand. We know that you feel as hot as an oven, that you're burning up with desire, that all you can think about is him.

But it's time to apply a little maths here.

From the day you officially start dating your lover you've got a clear four weeks of bad, smug, love-sick puppy behaviour.

You can giggle in public over every text he sends you, show us those little phone pictures of each other in bed and your workmates will forgive you if you sit there doing bugger-all work as you send each other emails ending in 'xxxxxxxxxxxxx'.

After the four weeks is up, take some style tips from your fridge and cool down a little, missy. You're boring us now. Your single friends would like a topic of conversation other than Him occasionally, so please stop shoehorning your boyfriend into every sentence. And frankly those pictures of him you've been showing off on your phone are starting to make us want to throw up.

If your girlfriends are true girlfriends they've probably not had the heart to tell you, but we bet that if you're in love you've been behaving pretty badly towards the sisterhood. Have a read through this chapter – it's time you pulled your stockings up and paid us some attention.

Here's what's acceptable within the first four weeks of your relationship. We call it The Four Week Rule.

The Four Week Rule

✓ *It's OK to send us those texts about him which are so long that they end *some text missing*.*

✓ You can leave us phone messages about him which are so long that you get interrupted by an automated voice saying 'you have ten seconds remaining'. Do bear in mind that no one actually has the time to listen to your long boring droning messages, so if you've got something important to say, like you're pregnant, then get it in during the opening ten seconds. Also if you get cut off because your message was so long, then don't for Chrissakes ring back and say, 'Oh. That was me,' and then carry on with another epic drone.

✓ You can forward all his email messages to us, and around the office, along with endless angsty questions to analyse what he's said and whether he's in love with you. You are entitled to waste up to half an hour each working day with this nonsense.

✓ You can point to various rashes on your chin and proudly say they are from stubble/the carpet/the sand (if you live near a beach).

✓ You can repeatedly tell us all about your first snog. (NB: First kiss details only, please. We're all excited for you on this one but frankly we don't want to be contacted every time you get a bit of action. And we don't want to know intimate details of your first night together. Unless, of course, it went horribly wrong in which case we can thoroughly enjoy poring over all the details.)

✓ If it's requested – and please don't do this uninvited – you can show us any pictures of him that you have in your mobile phone or on email. No nude pictures, please. Unless he has any medical anomalies which could spark an interesting discussion.

Sisterhood Cancellations

The decision of whether to choose The Shag or The Sisterhood for the evening is a minefield. Read through this whole section very carefully before picking up that phone to cancel the girls.

CANCELLING THE GIRLS FOR THE MAN – THE MATHS
In the first TWO WEEKS of this honeymoon period you can cancel a date with your girlfriends providing you play by the following rules:

1) **You are honest.** You must admit that the reason you are blowing them out is that you prefer the offer of meat and two veg with him over pizza Quattro stagione from her. Don't lie and say you're stuck at work – you'll just end up boasting about your big night out to someone later on and get caught out.

2) If you are blowing out a girlfriend you were planning to meet on her own you must give her *three days' notice*. Especially if it's the weekend. It is unacceptable to blow her out on the day, leaving her to sit on her own on a Friday night with nothing to do other than think of you having rampant sex. Be firm and say no to the man if he doesn't meet this three-day deadline. Trust us on this. Any man who wants to book you for the weekend should be booking you at least three days in advance and not just assuming you're going to be free. You'll look way too keen if you go and it's perfectly obvious you are willing to drop anything to be with him.

3) If you were planning a night out in a bar or restaurant with the girls as a group it is acceptable to blow them out the night before providing it is not a special celebration. Be honest though. And bear in mind they will spend the entire evening

slagging you off. If you had planned to cook for them all, however, it is unacceptable to cancel them and you will just have to get out of your little love nest, pop down to the supermarket and magic up a lovely dinner like you promised.

If, after two weeks has passed, your date asks you to blow out the girls and join him instead, you must say the following, 'I'd love to see you but I've already arranged an unbreakable date with my girlfriends. Hey, you're welcome to come along though and why not bring along a date for them? Do you have any fit, single, show-stoppingly handsome mates?' This is **true sisterhood behaviour** and a sure-fire way to make the girls fall for your new man. Any man who brings along a present like that for the others will be immediately accepted into your group.

CANCELLING THE MAN FOR THE GIRLS

If your girlfriends are going through any of the following crisis situations you should be there, in person, immediately. It doesn't matter what time of day or night it is or what country you're in. Tell her you'll be at her side as soon as you can, and mean it. Even if you're just about to have sex with someone wonderful for the first time. Of course, it goes without saying that you go round on your own. Your girlfriend's in trauma – the last thing she wants is to meet your new man right now.

1) *Emergencies*: Attempted suicide, relapses, unexpected bun in the oven. What are you reading us for? Get round there.
2) *Deaths*: Of family, friends, or adored celebrity icon (A-list only). With pets it isn't always necessary to take

immediate action. Mammals, i.e. cats, dogs and horses, should be dealt with asap and in person. With amphibian pet deaths, an order with Interflora is perfectly sufficient. Goldfish deaths really only merit a sympathetic phone call. They die all the time.

3) *Missing items*: Missing family treasures after break-ins and missing periods need immediate personal attention. If they're ringing to say they missed their train, flight or the airline's lost their luggage, be sympathetic. Offer help or a loan, but if they keep whingeing on about it, then advise them not to travel commercial in future and hang up. Missed periods should be dealt with immediately and in person. A true friend visits Boots on the way.

4) *Breakages*:

a) *Broken fashion items*: If we're talking designer, then broken heels hurt just as much as broken hearts. Jimmy Choos, Westwoods, Laboutins or Manolo Blahniks warrant immediate response, armed with superglue. Likewise if they're ringing to report any damage to couture. You should go round to sympathise and see if there's any way of hiding the damage. If it's only a high street brand tell them to get over it.

b) *Broken limb*: Broken legs, ankles, backs, necks or noses also require immediate attention. If they can still walk, breathe unaided and have been able to reach the phone to ring you, offer to see them later in the week. Check if they need an ambulance first, though, they will appreciate the thought.

c) *Broken heirlooms*: If they've just broken something really expensive then there's no need to go over either. Tell them to try Google to assess the damage and offer to watch *Bargain Hunt* in the morning to spot any possible replacements.

5) *Collapse*: Of relationships. Or noses. Deal with immediately and in person. (A collapsed soufflé is not worth an immediate call-out. Tell them to ring Harrods and get another one delivered.)

6) *Dumped*: Be by their side immediately if the relationship has lasted longer than three months. Any relationship which was shorter than three months can be dealt with by an immediate sympathetic phone call and a promise to meet in a few days' time. If it's a bun in the oven situation too, you need to call a cab.

7) *Loss, of virginity or weight*: Presumably this is a cause for celebration? Why are they ringing to say it's a crisis? Just say congratulations. There's absolutely no need to meet them outside WeightWatchers. Loss of job should be dealt with in person. Bring a bottle and the job section of the local paper.

Unacceptable Behaviour for Newly Loved-up Women

The following is unacceptable at any point. Even if you've only just met him:

1) Showing off those pictures of him that you keep in your wallet. Yeah, yeah. You've pulled. Just shut up about it, you smug cow. Remember, *wallet* equals *vomit*.

2) Having those patronising conversations to try and make your girlfriends feel better. You know, the ones where you look at us pityingly and say, 'Don't worry. I'm sure it'll just happen naturally for you one day.' And then suggest they go speed-dating. Or go to evening classes. Or go and look for people shopping for meals for one in supermarkets. Your girlfriends

are quite within their rights to call you a patronising old bag at this point and blank you for the rest of the evening.

3) Lying, for example, that things are, 'Oh, all right, you're not missing much'. Look, we know you're finally having rampant sex and are over the moon, and we'll forgive you seeing as it's all so new. Just don't bang on about it all night, OK?

4) Bringing him unannounced to a Girls Emergency Summit meeting to discuss a crisis such as an unexpected pregnancy. This is no time for smug couples. This is no time for men at all. The girls have booked you, and you on your own. They have been looking forward to a bitchfest about various love rivals, or deep discussions on gynaecology or a whinge about how they are manless. They will not appreciate an evening watching you two holding hands.

5) Telling us you've lost weight because lovemaking has used up so many calories is unforgivable, too. There's no need to rub our noses in it when we've been eating lentils and doing bloody aerobics all week and we're still as fat and single as ever.

CHECKLIST

The following is good sisterhood behaviour and, if possible, it would be good to achieve at least a couple during the Four Week Rule.

❑ *On a night with the girls, don't sit there looking smug, checking your phone messages and texting every two minutes. Switch off the phone and give them your full attention rather than making it perfectly obvious you wish you were elsewhere with him. Visit the loo and check your messages in private there, if you have to.*

❑ *Try asking them how they all are at some point during the evening.*

❑ *Don't mention the man until you're asked about him. And not doing that annoying thing of bringing him into every conversation, e.g. 'Oh, you want a glass of red wine? Nigel says that the thing about red wine is . . .'*

❑ *Pay full attention to their tales of doomed dates and don't get smug and say things like, 'Well, I don't think you should have slept with him on the first night.' Even if it's perfectly obvious that the man is never going to call because your friend has behaved like a slag/mad desperate woman you must give hope and reassure her that she's done nothing wrong, that he may call, but that he isn't good enough for her anyway. Just because you've got a man, don't start being superior or think you know it all. Remember, the girls guided you through every failed relationship you've ever had without making you feel bad about yourself.*

❑ *Give them some element of hope. Reiterate that you're going to ask your man if he's got any available single friends he can hook them up with. And genuinely do try and find them some single men, too. Remember, your priority now should be to fix up the others.*

❑ *Also try and bring along some examples of friends whose relationships are going really badly and who are now beginning to wish they'd never met the other person. Use celebrity examples if you have to. Just Google 'Heather Mills' for ideas.*

❑ *You could also drop in comments like how he messes up your flat or farts in bed so they can go back to their pristine Egyptian white cotton and feel smug. Don't overdo this though – they know you're having a fabulous time.*

❑ *Tell the girls you've got cystitis from all the sex. Back up your lie by ordering lots of vodka and cranberry juice and spending a long time in the loo. Wince frequently on your return.*

❑ *If there are any awkward silences, tell them that they've all lost weight and look fabulous.*

❑ *You should also look dog rough.*

Looking Dog Rough

It's important that you don't look that hot for your first post-coital meeting with the girls. They are already jealous of you and your amazing love life and you want to leave them feeling slightly superior and with something to bitch about the second you go off to the loo. Plus, you want them to feel better about being single. Do any of the following and your girlfriends won't mind the jolly smile on your face because they'll have one too.

We suggest saying that you've put on weight. Look, if you haven't just pretend, OK? They all presume you've been lying in bed feeding each other croissants and the girls will want something to make them feel better that all they've had to do in the evenings is go to a spin class on their own.

Dig out an outfit which is too small for you, or go out and buy one a size smaller than you are. As you turn up, say ruefully that you've put on weight as you haven't had time to get down to the gym and have been eating too many croissants, etc. Just before leaving the house, hack away at one of the buttons on your outfit so it's on its last thread and will then pop off the second you sit down. You can then do the embarrassed grin thing, ask if you can borrow a jumper off someone and spend the entire evening as a figure of fun, desperately holding her outfit together over her fat little tummy.

You should also look a bit tired and have dodgy skin. Now we know this is difficult because you've got that unmistakable glow — but don't worry, we've got some tips for you that'll help pull the cashmere over their eyes. Follow these and instead of hating you, the others will all be thinking, 'Poor thing, she may be getting it but she looks f***ing rough' and they'll all still love you.

◆ Get some of those blue eye-drops from the chemist that are designed to make your eyes look all sparkly after a big night out. Using your finger, apply a few drops directly on to the skin *under* your eyes. This will give you a bluey-grey pallor. (NB: Don't improvise with blue biro ink as it stains and it'll still be there the next day when you want to look your best for your man.) Then, over the top apply a shade of concealer which is a shade too light for you. This will draw attention to you while looking like you've really tried hard to cover it up.

◆ Don't wash your hair, so you look a bit lank and dull. Should you have any spots (which is highly unlikely given your happy circumstances), have a darn good squeeze before going through the door.

◆ Arrange for some sort of hideous rash on your face from all the snogging you've been doing. The girls will be delighted as well as comforted to see this unsightly reaction, and will enjoy an entertaining few minutes discussing their own rash/love-bite histories. This has the double effect of not only reassuring the girls that you look awful but also reminding them that they did have sex at some point in the past. If you don't have a rash, fake it. Should you opt for the ten-minute face-grounding into the carpet method, don't do it in a public place as it may well get caught on CCTV cameras and lead to a police interrogation. If you are a celebrity we would also advise against doing this on any red carpet as it could result in embarrassing paparazzi footage. If it's an emergency, you could rub a clothes brush over your face but it's not as effective.

Do any or all of these, turn up and moan that you look dreadful. The girls, if they are true friends, will all tell you that you look fabulous and give you a hug. OK, it's little white lies all round but everyone's happy this way, especially the girls.

The Bad Behaviour of Couples

If you have a lover then sit down with him and look through this checklist and ask yourself honestly if you've ever done any of the following. If you have then **stop it**. We'll tell you how to deal with it later on.

CHECKLIST

❑ *You turn up at a dinner party with one bottle of wine. From 'Us'. You tight-fists. How would you feel if a singleton friend turned up on your doorstep with one of those miniature bottles of wine you get on planes? A man should really be gallant enough to suggest he takes his own gift to a dinner party, but don't bank on it. Basically, it's down to the woman to take control at this point. You should make sure you turn up with two bottled alcoholic offerings. At least. If anything, go over the top and bring three. And flowers. OK, it costs you more, but you're the ones getting it regularly so it's a small price to pay.*

❏ *You buy one birthday present from 'Us'. And one Christmas present. And yet I bet you fully expect two presents in return, don't you? This sort of pitiful one-present offering is only acceptable if the gift is f***ing good. Couture, we'd say. One Jimmy Choo shoe from each of you would be just fine. Remember, if it's joint, it's got to be designer.*

❏ *Sending Christmas cards with photographs of yourselves embracing. Who do you think you are? Mary and Joseph? Don't do it – it looks naff. Unless of course you're royalty. We love getting Christmas card photographs from royalty.*

❏ *If sharing a flat with a single person, do not cook elaborate sexy dinners for two on the nights when the other person is in unless you intend to offer to let them eat with you. There is nothing worse as a singleton than having to wait three hours for you to cook your bloody lobster thermidor before we get a chance to go in there and put our ready-made pizza for one in the oven.*

❏ *Holding hands during dinner parties, calling each other pet nicknames in public and playing footsie under the table is one hundred per cent out of order. Remember, when you go to a dinner party, the hostess will have spent hours slaving over everything. They, and their food, should be the focus of attention, not you two making everyone vomit by cooing nonsense like, 'Hello my little Love Teddy' across the table.*

❏ *It's also really bad form to insult your hostess by making it perfectly obvious you'd much rather be under the duvet and eating pizza in bed than making polite conversation over her canapés.*

❏ *It is, of course, totally unacceptable to bonk in the hostess's bed during the course of dinner, or arrange to meet for a quick one in her bathroom. This is just rubbing everybody's face in it and you deserve to be struck off the dinner party invite list for ever. Or get some sort of rash. We deal with how to have sex in someone else's home politely on page 112.*

❏ *No public displays of affection please. TPT don't like PDA. And SM says no Se3M by the ATM. In other words, just a quick kiss on greeting will suffice. There's no need to start eating each other in public. It is totally unacceptable to hold hands and start kissing during a dinner party. Instead, you should restrict yourself to mouthing 'You OK?' at occasional intervals, straightening his collar a couple of times, maybe ruffling his hair. If you really wanted to spend the whole night indulging in PDAs then you should never have accepted the invitation. Of course, if any of your friends has been recently dumped, you should not hold hands with your man, you should not kiss at any point and you shouldn't betray even the slightest hint that you are enjoying an active sex life. If possible, you shouldn't really bring him at all.*

❑ *If you do feel the urge to embrace, volunteering to wash up is a nice gesture and can lead to some quality snogging time in the kitchen. We're sorry but you will have to wash up at some point.*

❑ *Do not discuss any embarrassing sex incidents involving your single friends in front of your man, ever. In public you must make out that they are all fabulous wanton sex kittens that any of his single friends would be proud to date. Never, ever let him think they are manless and sad.*

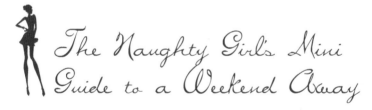

The Naughty Girl's Mini Guide to a Weekend Away

Of course, during a weekend away we don't expect you to behave like a nun. Your girlfriends will probably provide a double bed for you. If she's just been dumped horribly then maybe you should try and refrain from having fabulous sex all night but, let's face it, wine will have been consumed the previous evening so it's entirely likely that you will end up behaving like bunnies.

Do remember the sisterhood, though, and play by the following rules if possible.

1) How many times must we say this? No heavy petting in public, please. It is permissible to sit on his knee or give each other shoulder massages, but only at the end of the evening,

when everyone else is hammered, or when you are absolutely certain everyone else is tucked up in bed as well.

2) Show some respect. Any lovemaking which takes place in your room should be done on the floor. The carpet will deaden all sound, and nobody wants to hear your bedsprings creaking all night. Maybe this is the time to experiment doing it in the bath/shower if you have an en suite. If there's no shower and the floorboards creak consider a walk outside to romp al fresco. Watch out for any movement-sensitive lighting. You don't want to be lit up like Blackpool Illuminations outside their garage door.

3) If you really are a noisy little shrieker and you know you'll end up shouting the house down, then plan ahead. Pre-record yourselves having a massive row. Suggested topics: 'I

definitely saw you flirting with him/her' or 'What do you mean, she's a better cook than me?' Remember to make it realistic and put in plenty of door slamming for good measure. Play the tape at full volume and it will drown out the sounds of your lovemaking. Any screams of ecstasy at this point will simply sound like part of the row. Remember to make love on the carpet, as the sounds of you screaming combined with the thud of the bedstead hitting the wall will make them think you're being beaten up and come running in together.

The pair of you pairing hammer-and-tongs backed by a pre-recorded row at full volume just may take some explaining.

CHECKLIST
- [ ] *His job is to charm all the girls in the morning. We suggest he comes armed with enough food to cook everybody a darn good fry-up, which should be delivered to each of their doors, complete with a cup of tea and assurance that hey, they look great!*
- [ ] *If you have broken any golden rules the night before – like engaging in public snogging – then try and make amends by paying some sort of forfeit, like going out and getting the newspapers.*
- [ ] *If you were caught sleeping in her bed, then this is an absolute insult to your hostess, especially if she is single. He should consider an immediate emergency gift purchase. A Chloé handbag is always nice.*
- [ ] *Do check that you have absolutely got rid of any evidence of your fantastic night of sex. Your friends should not be expected to spend the next day picking up knickers or any other evidence from the floor.*

❏ *Do not turn up the next morning half-dressed and holding hands, and say, 'Oh, sorry, hope we didn't keep you all awake last night.' You've already ruined everyone's night. There's no need to be so smug about it and ruin the next morning as well.*

Remember, revel in your happiness, you lucky old tart. But don't rub everyone else's noses in it.

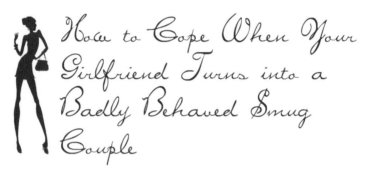

How to Cope When Your Girlfriend Turns into a Badly Behaved Smug Couple

If your girlfriend has turned into one half of a Smug Couple, then your best bet is to be as charming as possible on the surface. Try and be pleased for her that she's going through this wonderful flush of romance. Deal with the fact that she's being a selfish cow about it by being cool and looking unfazed. You can always bitch about her behind her back to your other girlfriends later.

Remember, eventually she'll realise what she's doing and come back to planet Earth. Meanwhile sit yourself next to him at parties, be encouraging, warm and welcoming. Rise above it.

BE EMPOWERED.

Talk to yourself in the mirror before they arrive and tell yourself you're going to look delighted for them and their perfect life of physical fulfilment. And don't mind in the slightest that she's going to practically have sex in front of you all night. Make him love you as much as he loves her. If you create a barrier between you and her man you risk losing her altogether and she'll go off in her little pink cloud convinced you're in the wrong.

Your girlfriends are friends for life and you must forgive their little shortcomings. And she's not the first to behave this way. Why do you think so many people are reading this book? That said, it doesn't mean you don't get your own back if they've committed any of the Smug Couple Crimes:

Here's the checklist and how to get your own back.

CHECKLIST
☐ *Feel no remorse in using ruthlessness to deal with stinginess. If they turn up with just a single bottle of wine at a dinner party, say thank you, accept it and then stand there pointedly holding out your hand for the other bottle. When it doesn't materialise, make a great fuss of 'how expensive' the one bottle they've bought is. Put it in pride of place – especially if it's something that cost under a fiver. Having thus exposed them, punish further by giving them just one glass between them. Wait until they ask for another, then smile sweetly and say, 'Oh, I'm sorry. I didn't realise you were both drinking.' Then look pointedly at their pathetic one bottle offering. With luck he should be shamed into asking for the location of the*

nearest Threshers. Show no embarrassment in issuing directions and make no attempt to stop him going.

❏ If they persist in giving one present from 'Us' and yet hold separate birthday parties to which you are excepted to arrive armed with individual presents then simply retaliate by giving crap gifts. One sock each at Christmas should get the message across. Keep doing this until their gifts improve.

❏ Don't ever share a flat with a couple. If a perfectly nice flatmate turns into a Smug Couple then just simply try and split up the selfish pigs – see page 176 for hints.

❏ If a couple are always lovey-dovey over dinner then split them up when they come round. Seat a person in between them so they have to make conversation with someone else rather than coo at each other. If you're forced to put them opposite each other, try to assess in advance if their legs will be long enough to play footsie under the table. If you suspect they will be trying to have secret sex during your dinner then simply put obstacles under the table like wine bottles or dogs. These will make a loud noise should there be any furtive fumbling. The whole table will then go quiet and stare at the culprits and you can make a huge fuss clearing up broken bottles or angry dogs and telling them not to worry about it.

❏ If a couple persist in heavy petting in public then invite them round with all your friends who are on a diet. They will all be put off their food and feel like vomiting and really thank you for it when they get on the scales the next morning.

❏ If they do completely ruin your evening and destroy your soul then do not cry in front of them. Ever. Even if they *are making you feel awful, lonely and sad. If you feel a bit maudlin, go out and give yourself a stiff talking-to in front of the mirror and tell yourself she'll come back to the fold soon.*

❑ *Just keep repeating the mantra in your head that you're happy to be single. Make up lots of men who are after you, pretend to look at text messages, have men's underwear lying around. In short, do anything to pretend you're having a fabulous time of your life and their selfish Smug Couple behaviour does not bother you in the slightest. If it's among a group of girlfriends then make sure you all read this chapter in advance so that no one looks surprised at this sudden talk of mystery boyfriends.*

Our best advice is that you simply go and put this book on the bathroom floor. Open at page 96. Incidentally, if this is where you came in we do hope you've got the hint and it's now time to get off the loo, go and rejoin your girlfriends and start to make amends. If we were you we'd go via Threshers or Cartier on the way.

PART TWO

The Naughty Girl's Guide to Style

THE STYLE MANTRA:

*Grant me the serenity to never wear pop socks –
even if they are under boots and people cannot see them*

*Courage to realise that I do have cellulite and should
dress accordingly*

*And the wisdom never to buy anything that is a size too
small, even if it is in the sale, and I really am going
to start that new diet soon.*

Of course there's no point us teaching you how to have a fabulous sex life and be an amazing member of the sisterhood if you then go and ruin it by wearing the wrong outfit. So here's our guide on what to wear.

The Naughty Girl in Wardrobe

It doesn't matter if your budget is Prada or Primark. Never part with a penny unless you're absolutely convinced that what you've got will make you hot to trot for the task ahead.

You need to think about so much more than whether your outfit makes your bottom look big. The stylish naughty girl needs to be ready for every eventuality. Here's what you need to think about.

First Dates

With any outfit you choose for a first date, you must first check the store gives refunds. Say you need to check if the outfit matches your Choos, and then take it home.

Once home, think about what your first date is likely to entail and then re-enact the situation to see how good you look. A little judicious testing now will save you all manner of embarrassment later on. For example, say he's going to be driving you home. It's entirely likely that you will want to snog him just as he drops you at your door. Practise. Put your outfit on then position a full-length mirror in front of your sofa at home. Sit coyly on it, leaning one hand on an imaginary gearstick as you practise leaning over for your kiss.

Study yourself in the mirror. How does it look? If you can, position a video camera where he'll be sitting and then playback to see what he'll be seeing. When you go to kiss him, does the top fall open in an inviting direction? Is the waistband flexible enough to be grabbed in closer? Do your thighs look elephantine in that skirt?

Check the mirror. Can you exit the car with dignity or will your knickers be on full display as you get out? Practise sliding off the sofa to find out. As a general rule it's no to sports skirts in sports cars.

Your gusset should never be seen on a first date.

Look around your house and improvise. If he drives a Lamborghini, you'll have to rehearse this move on something low like a coffee table. If he's in a Range Rover go for something like a washing machine (put it on spin dry if you're planning on having a few drinks). A futon will do for a Ferrari. A bidet will double as a motorbike. If the date is likely to be riding a horse, maybe try straddling an ironing board.

Re-enact your whole date if necessary. Sipping cocktails, replacing divots at a polo match, boarding a private jet, running along the beach of his private island hideaway, going for a kebab. Whatever you have in mind. Check how the outfit will look at every stage.

NB: If the store does not allow refunds you'll simply have to experiment on the shop floor. Improvise with checkout counters, display stands, or whatever's or whoever's available. Some of the more prestigious department stores should be able to provide washing machines and coffee tables to practise on. Otherwise just go to Harrods – they can probably get you the Lamborghini and the horse if you give them enough notice.

If you're buying an outfit with a sexual encounter in mind, it would be considered bad manners to rehearse any part of this activity in the middle of the shop floor. Especially in Harrods. And besides, nobody likes a show-off. Go home and swing from your own chandeliers.

First Time Sex

We're not against one-night stands, girls, but do bear in mind that sometimes it's better to wait. Not because you're trying to pretend you're a lady. But because there's so much preparation involved in dressing for that successful first time.

Pick an outfit that lends itself to stockings or hold-ups and dress accordingly. Trust us. Things will go entirely differently if you've got sexy hosiery on. If you're trussed up in full-strength deniers and sweaty before you've even left the front door, what possible chance do you have of convincing him you're the most desirable being on the planet?

If you don't believe us, try putting the pair of tights over your head before you go out. See how bad you look. Do it. This is important. Now do you really intend on going out like that? And do you really think he'll go for you?

The rule with dressing for sex is that a man does not want everything on a plate. He wants to imagine what's in the box, so to speak.

Imagine you're sitting on the beach. The girls sitting there in cute bikinis leave more to the imagination than those going topless and letting it all hang out. So, conceal. Suggest. Let him think there's a whole load of fabulous things nestling under that outfit that he, lucky boy, may just get to explore if he plays his cards right.

Don't whack it all out on display. Of course, an added advantage of conceal and suggest is that you can shove a load of padding down your front and make him think there's a lot more down there than there really is.

Of course, the problem with all this extra padding is that, all being well, you're going to have to be taking it off in front of someone later on. Practise the following at home until you've got it perfect. Always remove your bra and all underlying padding/chicken fillets/socks in one swift move. Girls, if you've gone for an artificial boost in your bra, you're going to have to take control of the undressing. There's no use letting him sexily unhook your bra and then have everything thud to the floor. It'll just ruin the moment.

So, just say, 'Let's get out of these.' Cup one arm across the front of your bra and its hidden extras, unhook at the back with the other hand and in one swift movement shove everything quickly to the floor.

Then leap on him and distract him.

NB: Be careful that the chicken fillets don't fly out of your hands like a Frisbee and whack against the bedroom window. If one of them does, just giggle, say, 'Darn those pigeons!' and jump on top of him as quickly as you can before he has time to think about it. For more tips on being naked – see page 90.

Meeting the Future In-Laws

Cover all cleavage and accessorise with a gift. We suggest flowers or a scented candle. And, afterwards, a handwritten thank you letter. In ink. Especially if you're writing to peers or royal personages. They hate letters written in biro.

Work

It depends on whether you're skiving off or not – see page 136 for more details.

Buying a Bikini

Most girls mess this up. They pick the bikini in the prettiest colour, pop it on, and look at their reflection in the changing room mirror for about five seconds before deciding to buy it. Then they can't work out why they look so different in the holiday photographs.

When buying and wearing a bikini, don't think of it as a bikini. Think of it as a pair of knickers and a bra. A pair of knickers and a bra that you are about to wear in public and be photographed in.

If you were told that tomorrow you had to go to work in nothing but your pants and the whole thing was to be captured on film, you'd spend a lot of time making sure you had on the most flattering option available. You would think big pants – not pretty little things with tiny weeny strips of material and pretty braids. You would think underwired bras which are the geniuses of lifting, separating and thrusting. Do the same amount of planning for your bikini.

Just because your inhibitions have gone it doesn't mean your cellulite will have.

Obviously you're not going to spend your entire holiday standing up and admiring yourself in mirrors, so you need to work out what that bikini will look like in action.

1) Push your tummy out. Yes. We knew you were breathing in. But you can't breathe in for a two-week holiday, can you? Now imagine you've eaten pasta and ice cream every day and push it out some more. There. Maybe a sarong *would* be a good idea.

2) Turn away from the mirror and imagine picking up an object from the floor. Pause and look back mid-action. What does your behind look like? Is there anything showing that might frighten small children?

3) Wave frantically at an imaginary friend in the surf. Does anything pop out? Or flop out?

4) Jump up and down and pretend to play volleyball.

5) Lie on your back and writhe around on the floor as if you were snogging a fabulous holiday lover on a sun lounger. Check out the mirror to see how you look mid-wriggle.

6) Avoid novelty clasps. Men are simple creatures. Your bikini should be too. He will be easily confused if presented with anything marginally more complex than a bra clasp. Pop your head out of the changing room curtain and if there's a good-looking man around you can always invite him in to see what he thinks.

7) Beware of details like beading. They may look fabulous, but they can get caught on people, sun beds, seaweed or sea creatures. Models have beading on their swimsuits all the time, but they're usually travelling with an entourage and working with a highly trained team from *Vogue* who can look out and check for dangers. Try it. Writhe around on the carpet and see if bits of your bikini get stuck to it. If you're in a department store with a fish counter maybe pop down in your bikini and ask if you can practise brushing against the sea creatures in your cozzie and see if

anything gets caught. Emerging from the sea with the entire cast of *Finding Nemo* clinging to your rear is not a good look.

8) Think of the tan lines. Even if a bikini is fabulous and you look really hot in it, stay clear if it's got odd cutaway holes and weird straps and things. You might look good in it on holiday but it's not practical to keep wearing the bikini in the office when you get home.

9) Throwing water over yourself will probably be frowned upon, even in the most understanding of department stores, but we do suggest that before taking your bikini on holiday you do a little extra research at home. Lie down in the bath and then quickly stand up in your bikini - does it fall down to your knees when wet? If you're flat-chested and have gone for heavy padding, do the all-important lumps of material stay in place?

10) What will it look like when you emerge from the surf? Jump around in it a bit when it's wet. Does it still hold in everything it was meant to hold in? Does it go see-through? Are you going to need extra waxing to wear this?

There are a lot of things to think about but don't get paranoid and depressed about bikini purchasing.

Nobody looks good in a bikini and those model pictures are all airbrushed anyway.

Besides, we're going to teach you a few beach tricks on page 204 that'll ensure you always look stunning on the sands.

Alternatively, you could just go skiing instead.

Yachts

Don't bother investing in expensive shoes if you're going on a yacht. It's etiquette to remove your shoes before boarding. Even really nice ones. So spend on the rest of the outfit instead. If you're on Valentino's yacht the interior is navy and white – so dress to tone.

Polo

Go for wedges, rather than stilettos. Girls who run out to replace the divots in spindly heels look stupid and tarty. And everyone sneers at them knowing they haven't got a clue.

Aeroplanes

If flying by private jet (see page 85 for hitch-hiking tips) do not wear a pencil skirt as they're a bugger when boarding. If you're aiming for allure in a Lear then wear beige to biscuit cashmere accessories as these will perfectly match the interior. Incidentally, only do this trick on private jets as they tend to be a lovely pale colour. If you're flying easyJet, we heartily recommend you don't try and match the orange livery. It won't do your complexion any favours.

Even if you're skint, you should never fly without chic luggage. Shabby chic is fine and second-hand will cost you next to nothing. If there's a monastery in your holiday destination then pop in. The monks arrive with their luggage cases and then never leave, and you can go in and ask for them. TPT's friend once got a set of fabulous vintage suitcases off some Tibetan novices.

Fancy Dress

If you go out in fancy dress do check if the outfit is functional for an emergency overnight stay. Tara once got arrested after a party in Germany, while dressed as a rabbit and spent a very uncomfortable night on a bench with her bunny tail digging right in. Likewise, a friend of ours was locked out of his flat dressed as a Smurf and fell attempting to climb up to the second-floor window. A five-hour wait on a hospital trolley is bad enough, but so much worse when you're dressed solely in underpants and blue paint. Do check your outfit for all eventualities.

Pop Stars

As these are a speciality of TPT's, here are some extra tips. If you get to meet them, don't sit there with everything hoisted up and on display. Pop stars spend their days surrounded by writhing dancers in tight leotards and having people scream at them for sex. You've got to go for a different approach. *Cover up, keep your breasts warm for later and you'll stand out.*

Weddings

Remember, the bigger and grander the church, the colder it will be in there. They may be red-hot in love at the front but it's jolly chilly at the back. At the most recent royal wedding, for example, it was freezing, but happily Tara was able to hand out spare warm undergarments to many grateful members of the congregation so they could all enjoy the glorious service in comfort.

At the most recent royal wedding, for example, it was freezing, but happily Tara was able to hand out spare warm undergarments to many grateful members of the congregation so they could all enjoy the glorious service in comfort.

Hats are good. They set off the outfit and look fantastic. Just watch the size of the brim. You're not Alexis Carrington Colby. Think of the people sitting behind. Try and kiss your reflection in the mirror before you leave.

If the only way you can reach it is by twisting your head to an awkward angle then the brim is too large and it will become a real obstacle kissing the guests hello (or the best man good night). It will also give you an obscene headache.

Obviously don't wear white – not even if you don't like the bride. It just looks cheap. Nothing paler than light biscuit, please.

Funerals

Think Jackie O. She was always going to funerals and always looked ravishing. And think about it, she never dated less than a billionaire. The trick is not to make the outfit too sexy. Even if there are hot men among the mourners you should show respect and go for a demure frontage. Remember, black is slimming so you can compensate by going for something slightly more fitted than normal. Always take a spare pair of stockings in your handbag so you can change for the wake if you need to. There's a grave risk of ladders with all that up and down in the splintery pews, and they are so much more noticeable with black hosiery.

Shoulder Pads

A complete fashion faux pas these days. But, don't fret. If you have accidentally bought something which is padded at shoulder level then you haven't wasted your money. Simply unpick them carefully and stick them in your bra instead. Or on your buttocks. Wherever you need a boost.

Pastels

The only person in history who could really pull off pastels, ever, was the Queen Mother. The rest of us should just stay clear. You'll end up wandering around like a giant Neapolitan ice cream and not look remotely sweet to the opposite sex. The only possible exceptions are Chanel twinsets.

Polyester

No. No matter how cheap it is. Or how well cut. You will sweat like a little piggy and get those great big rings round your armpits. Not a great look.

Stone-washed Denim

Oh, please. You may as well have thrown up on your pants. The only exception to this rule is if you are a member of Status Quo. Actually, if you are a member of Status Quo, we think it's time you moved on too.

Tie-dye

T-shirts with the 'interesting' speckled effect of dye patterns are a no-no. We've seen some really quite expensive ones on rather good-looking men and women. It never works. It just looks like you've dribbled something down your front. Go for plain colours.

Knickers

Wear some. There are far too many starlets out there at the moment being snapped commando. That's not naughty. It's nasty. Remember, it's pants to wear no pants. To be honest, even just wearing a G-string is pretty bad.

Tights

As we've said before, it's never really acceptable to wear thick woollen tights.

Whatever you buy, it'll never look stylish unless it fits. Be honest with yourself. What size are you really?

The idea of Lycra, for example, is that it helps a garment skim sensuously across your curves. It is not meant to be clinging on for dear life and ripping apart at the seams. Put on your trousers and ask yourself if you look sexy. Or if you look like a sofa. If the look is veering towards DFS then always go one size up. You can always cut out the label and lie. For diet tips see page 261.

PART THREE:

The
Naughty Girl
at Work

Tara slept throughout the writing of this section. The nearest she's
been to the office is the office party.

PRAYER

*Grant me the serenity to realise that the
so-called Big Cheese is a mere triangle of Dairylea
in the cheeseboard of life.*

*Courage to realise that the worst that can happen
is a P45. And a lie-in.*

*And the wisdom to be nice to all my family, and
also all old people with posh watches, in the hope
that an inheritance will come my way so I can just
quit the job tomorrow.*

The Naughty Girl's Guide to the Office

How to Pull a Sickie

We've worked for some real jerks in the past. One of Sharon's bosses would have a hissy fit if the staples in his documents weren't at a precise ninety-degree angle to the corner of the paper. And he used to kick a football at your head during tellings-off.

If your boss makes every working day a nightmare then, in the interests of good karma, you should have some nice time off at their expense.

The following method of pulling a sickie is used by household names on TV- and movie-sets all the time. Use it in your office. It will not only get you time off, it will be guilt-free and leave you looking like an absolute hero.

Total number of days you've been employed by the idiot ÷ 91 = days you are entitled to skive off.

Or – put simply – we'd say you should pull four sickies per year of miserable service.

(Listen, if you really hate your job, take these sickies, start sending out your CV and look on the bright side. Once you've factored in your holiday leave, bank holidays, tube strikes, genuine illnesses, Christmas, doctor's appointments, dentist visits, lunch breaks and fag breaks, this adds up to barely any time in the office at all. On the rare occasions you do actually find yourself behind your desk, you can then simply offer to do a tea/fag run to get out again.)

The most important thing about conning your boss is that you must plan ahead. Decide exactly how much time off you'd like to have and then prepare your fake illness accordingly.

As a guide, it's always best to take at least two days off sick to make things more believable.

Lots of people claim they've had a 'twenty-four-hour flu bug' and are back at the office all perky the next morning. But let's face it, whenever anybody says this it's pretty obvious that they just couldn't be arsed coming in and they weren't the tiniest bit ill.

Shorter periods away can be done on an ad hoc basis. If you just need an extra hour to pick out a fabulous pair of shoes in the sales, then simply exit the office, leaving your computer switched on, a file open on screen and your jacket over the back of the chair. Switch your phone to silent so nobody notices that you're not picking up. Do this just after lunch and don't say goodbye to anyone or draw attention to your exit.

If anyone asks for you in your absence, your colleagues will look, see the evidence and automatically report that 'her computer's on/jacket's still here so she must be around'. If you've got an understanding colleague you can also arrange for them to keep putting half-empty cups of hot coffee next to the keyboard for added authenticity.

Nine times out of ten, people won't even notice you've gone. If they do, just say you took 'a late lunch'. This technique also works well if you wish to leave the office at 3 p.m. Simply leave the jacket and computer overnight. The added bonus is that if your boss does a late-night swoop of the office, he will assume you are also beavering away and burning the midnight oil. It will also make it look like you were first into the office the next day.

If you need an emergency morning off simply ring in, sigh and say, 'The flat above me has been burgled and they need everyone to stay in the building for statements.' This will buy you a lie-in until lunchtime. Trust us. It always works.

(Incidentally, to everyone we've worked for who is thinking this excuse sounds a little familiar then we would like to assure you that we were telling the truth. Honest.)

One Week Before

Start giving some thought to which affliction you intend to have. Maybe Google a few ideas and look up symptoms on medical sites. Keep it simple. Don't go for things like dengue fever, flesh-eating viruses or herpes as these will make you the subject of office gossip.

A simple chest infection is always good. A fever with a high temperature will get you up to three days off. For five days off, aim for a stomach upset but be prepared – you'll be expected to embellish with sordid details such as, 'Oh my God, it was gushing like water, as though a champagne cork had popped.'

You can, at this stage, start claiming to feel 'ropey'. Keep quiet about any plans for big nights out during your intended time off. If the boss even remotely suspects you're about to attend a round of fabulous parties and get lots of lie-ins at his expense, you'll never get away with it.

The idea of preparing the ground well in advance is to turn things to your advantage. Instead of being seen as a potential skiver, you must present as the complete workhorse, dragging yourself to the office when you're definitely one degree under.

If you intend to go down the stomach upset route, now is the time to mention that your entire deep freeze has gone into meltdown during a power cut and you're not quite certain what's safe to eat or not.

Two Days Before

Smother yourself in Tiger Balm, Vicks Vapour Rub or something that smells a mile off. People will begin to comment and you will reply weakly that, 'Yes, I think I have a cold coming on.'

Decide to eat the defrosted smoked haddock.

The Day Before

Remember that the day before your sick leave it is absolutely vital to ensure you get maximum sympathy and minimum suspicion from your office colleagues. You want them to fight to protect you while they rally round congratulating you on making such a brave and valiant effort. You want it to be their idea that you go home. You encourage this by saying how rough you feel and how you're soooo worried you may be passing on these hideous germs to them. Very soon they'll want to protect themselves rather than protecting you.

Wear mismatching pastels and pale lipstick. Do not apply blusher. Take the lift to your office even if you're on the first floor. You must appear subdued, exhausted, listless. Do not answer when people say 'Good morning' to you. Instead, wait for them to greet you for a second time, then give a thin smile, rub your eyes in a distracted way, say hello and sigh. If they ask if you're OK, say, 'Yes. I just feel a bit tired, that's all.'

By eleven in the morning, if it's a freezing-cold day, start saying, 'Is it just me or is it hot in here?' and ask if people mind you putting the air con on for a bit. If it's the middle of a heatwave put a really big coat on.

If you've got hay fever and it's summer then lucky you – simply don't take any medication. Sneeze unhappily throughout the afternoon.

Buy yourself some lunch, then make sure everyone sees you leave all of it. (Of course, this is merely a stunt lunch. You have some big fat sandwiches hidden in your bag and wolf them down when no one's looking). At 2 p.m. pop into the loos, use a brand of menthol lip balm like Carmex and smear it under in your eyes so they go a bit red and swollen. (We know we keep going on about this, but it's because Tara used it in her Walker's crisps ads the whole time when she had to do a crying scene, so we know it really works. It only costs a few pounds and you can get it at all chemists, including Harrods.) Then, arrange to be within earshot of the boss and loudly ask a colleague if they have any Lemsip. For the next two hours bang on about how bad you feel. Say you feel like you're going to throw up. Drop things. Breathe heavily on people. Soon everyone will be fed up with you and start suggesting that you get out of their airspace.

Go by four o'clock at the latest. Make sure everyone hears you call for a taxi because you feel 'just drained' and 'can't face the tube/bus/train home'. Four o'clock is a late enough exit to have proved you have fought a martyr-like battle against your illness because you don't want to let anybody down. It also gives you ample time to go home, have a bath, take any hay fever medication you've missed and then get ready for a big night out.

NB: If you're going for the full five days' sick leave, you may wish to send a text at this stage informing a colleague that you are throwing up/have explosive diarrhoea. Send it to the least discreet member of the office. For added authenticity you may wish to throw in a line complaining about excessive taxi soilage charges.

The Next Morning

The next morning you must inform your boss by telephone that you're not coming in. Remember you have nothing to feel guilty about. You have fought this lurgy for two days and dragged yourself about the workplace. Now, at the insistence of your colleagues, you have finally succumbed as the illness takes over.

This call is crucial. Ensure that your voice is as croaky as possible. Do not, under any circumstances, utter a single word to anyone before picking up that receiver. Do not sing. Do not laugh. Don't even hum. Do not consume a hot beverage. You want to sound as rough as possible. If you don't smoke, consider starting.

We would also recommend – hangover permitting – that you set your alarm for 6 a.m. That way you can ring and leave a message before anyone actually gets into the office.

For a full five days we suggest you try something like this:

'Hi. It's me. I'm so sorry but I just feel really, really ill. I just don't think I can make it in. I have to stay close to a loo . . . (Pause) . . . Oh God, I've got so much work to do, though. Maybe when you get in you could (Pause, as if thinking) . . . bike my desk and computer over to me or something? I could try and do all the work later, when it eases up. (Now make your voice fade a little and ensure you can be heard dropping back against the pillows before gasping.) Ring. Or text me. Don't worry about waking me up. I'll keep the phone by the bed. I'm so sorry.' (Then maybe just the gentlest of groans before replacing the receiver but don't overdo it.)

This should work at a number of levels:

◆ You immediately wrong-foot them because they're clearly not even in the office yet and you're already calling from your sick bed worrying about the day's labour.
◆ You're volunteering a solution so that you can carry on working – although obviously it's so highly impractical to bike over a desk that they're never going to bother.

◆ You've said they can ring, yet made it clear that if they do they will be waking you from your deathbed.

Nine times out of ten they'll take the hint and just send a text telling you not to worry, that they don't want to wake you, that you sound dreadful and that you should just try and get some rest. If the phone does ring, do not answer it. Let it go to voicemail. If it is your boss saying that he's read this book too and he will bike around your entire office including your P45, then don't ring the heartless git back for at least three hours. Later, claim that you must have slept through the call because you were genuinely, really ill.

Your Return

Your behaviour on returning to the office is crucial. Do not brag to anyone about your freebie days off.

TRUST NO ONE. You will blow everything if you do.

If you have spent your sick days shopping, do not come in wearing your smart new clothes. Do not smile. Remember, you've been very, very ill. Ill people don't beam broadly. Most importantly, bear in mind that if you've been claiming a stomach upset you will need to look significantly thinner. You can't go in like a fat little Cheshire cat or it will be perfectly obvious that you've spent a blissful week sitting on the sofa shoving chocolate down your throat.

We suggest wearing clothes that are actually one size larger than normal. When anyone approaches to ask if you're feeling better, woefully pull out the waistband, demonstrate how baggy the clothes are and claim you've lost half a stone.

CHECKLIST

☐ *Remember to be 'ill' all the way out of the building, into the car, and, if it's the office's regular taxi firm, all the way to your front door. You could be watched and recorded at any stage.*

☐ *Be aware of any CCTV cameras and ensure you look ill when you're in front of them too. No punching the air and looking at spa brochures as soon as everyone's out of the office.*

☐ *If you've been faking a stomach bug then on the day of your return make a point of eating something 'really bland' like a baked potato.*

☐ *Do not treat yourself to a trip to the hairdresser's and an exciting new look – you were supposed to have been on your sick bed.*

☐ *Do not travel abroad during your sick leave. One, your phone's ringtone will register as an international dial tone when the office rings, and two, a tan is such a giveaway.*

☐ *Do not make any live TV appearances.*

☐ *If you're after six weeks off you could always fake a fall and arrange to be found lying with your legs back to front on the office floor. Then claim you've really 'hurt your back'. Again, remember to check for CCTV cameras when choosing the scene for this particular performance.*

Never feel guilty about pulling a sickie.

A rested and happy employee is a good employee. Every extra day you spend under that duvet is actually helping your boss. He should be grateful that you are thinking laterally.

If you are reading this book in bed, having just scored yourself a nice freebie week, then bravo! No doubt it'll be time for a spot of shopping soon but, in the meantime, why not pop us down for a sec and have a well-deserved power nap.

The Naughty Girl's Mini Guide to Partying

Grant me the serenity to accept the things I cannot change,
Courage to change the things I can,
And the wisdom to know the difference.

That's the actual addict's prayer. When it comes to alcohol, don't overdo it, sister.

If you're in AA then read this chapter with a superior smile because it no longer applies to you.

The Office Christmas Party

The following advice is a tried and tested method used by celebrities the morning after award ceremonies. Adapt it for the day after your office party.

First of all, we'd like you to remember that whatever you did last night is not your fault. It's your boss's fault.

Let us explain. Your boss provided a party. He provided a party with alcohol. It was your job to enjoy said party and consume the alcohol. You were merely fulfilling a job description.

Anyone who was sober enough to remember what you were doing and start criticising you for it should be reported *immediately* to their superiors for not giving the evening their full participation and support. And for being really, really boring.

Having said that, if you were really badly behaved it's entirely possible that you might be in for a bit of stick at the office today. Lie still under the duvet for a moment while we guide you through how to deal with everything.

What Happened?

The first thing you must do is **assess the damage**. Remain horizontal as you think. Recollect. Piece together the evening. What did you do?

Open your eyes. Can you gauge any clues from your immediate surroundings? Are you in a skip? Are you on an operating table? Do you recognise that ceiling?

If you're at home, well done. Look next to you. Is there anyone lying there? Look under the duvet. Is there anyone under there? If there is then maybe they can throw some light on things.

Mobile phones are good for clues. What's in the picture/video section? Did you make any late night calls or send any inappropriate texts to your boss? Are there any voicemail messages saying you've been fired? **Has anyone phoned you to say you've made front page of the *Sun*?**

What to Worry About

The following are bad things to do at parties:

- Inappropriate bodily emissions in an inappropriate place. If you were sick in the loo that's OK. Had consensual rumpy pumpy in private? Don't worry about it. You're good to go. Everything happened in an appropriate place and manner and no apology is needed. However, if, say, you threw up on the managing director's suit in the middle of the dancefloor, that's an example of an inappropriate emission. It's not good. Especially if the suit was tailor-made or couture.
- Indecent exposure. This is also bad (unless you're exceptionally well endowed and/or you've just invested in major cosmetic surgery).
- Arson isn't clever, either.
- If there is someone under the duvet and they are the boss's wife/husband that could be an issue too. If the boss is in there with you, however, then happy days. You are in for a pay rise. If you are in bed with your boss and his wife make it a large pay rise.

Physical Damage

Get up and look in the mirror. Is there any physical damage which will need disguising with clever accessories?

Check your neck for love-bites. One of the downsides of being a naughty girl and having men constantly kissing your neck is that some of them are overcome with the urge to brand you by leaving toothmarks. Don't ask us why they do it – perhaps it's like dogs with trees. All sorts of men are prone to leaving them. It wasn't long ago that Tara was smooching a very famous artist. He left his masterpiece on her neck the day before she was due on live TV. The quickest way to heal them – and carpet burns on your chin, incidentally – is to apply calamine lotion. This won't conceal it completely, the only way to do that is with a polo neck or a fashionable scarf. Tara selected a fine Hermes square in the end. And insisted on a sizeable discount on a rather nice piece of art for her flat.

Your Return to the Office

If you're getting flashbacks about embarrassing behaviour and you think you might be in a spot of bother, the best thing to do is call a cab. You must get to the office immediately. **If you're not there you will be gossiped about behind your back.**

Do not pull a sickie. It just delays everything. Your strategy should be to get in early, control the rumours and, if possible, try and find someone who was worse than yourself so you can all start talking about them instead.

Your one white hope is that perhaps everyone else was too drunk to remember it. You will know within three seconds of pushing open the office door whether this is the case.

If you are responsible for any embarrassing stains or spills on other people's clothes we recommend an immediate and fulsome apology together with an offer to dry-clean. Don't be offended if they come back with an angry ultimatum that you should also book into a clinic and dry out. Ruining designer clothes is not good. If it was only high street, tell them to get over it.

Move the conversation quickly on to someone else. If you were the worst-behaved person at the party simply make up something about someone who isn't in the office yet. Suggesting a lesbian liaison is always a good one – pick the two prettiest girls in the office and people will soon forget about what you did.

Remember to put on a concerned face and say that you think it's best all round if no one mentions anything to either girl as 'I've heard they're mortified and hoping no one noticed them.' That way – with a bit of luck – no one will bother to check it out.

CHECKLIST
- [ ] *Go for sympathy. Mumble the following: 'I'm so sorry. I was on medication and I shouldn't have mixed it with alcohol. I tried not to.'*
- [ ] *Claim you'd had bad news and were self-medicating with alcohol.*
- [ ] *Nobody will believe you if you say your drink was spiked.*
- [ ] *Cheer up. At least you're not pregnant.*
- [ ] *Might you be? The morning-after pill still works after seventy-two hours.*

As we said earlier, don't overdo the partying. A bottle of vodka is not really an acceptable light snack for a typical evening out. But the main thing about partying mishaps is that everybody goes through them at some point.

Forgive yourself. We've all been there.

Sharon once lost part of her front tooth doing the splits on a wall at Christmas. And, as we told you before, Tara's been arrested.

Remember that you'll only be a figure of fun until it's the next person's turn to disgrace themselves. See if anyone in the office is up for a hair of the dog at lunchtime and hopefully you'll get the office gossip moved on to them instead.

The Naughty Girl's Mini Guide to Staff

Tradesmen, masseurs, waiters, gynaecologists. Paying people for services brings all sorts of issues. Should you tip them? Should you sleep with them? Is it OK to fire them after you've slept with them?

Let us guide you through a few minefields.

Grant me the wisdom to realise that being rude to staff is particularly tacky,
Courage to know that sex with tradesmen leads to trouble. And doesn't get your pipes fixed,
And the wisdom to ask them out anyway – if they're really hot.

The most important rule is that you should always treat people in the way you wish to be treated. Don't be rude, don't humiliate and don't be flash. Remember that you may be paying people but really they're in charge.

Looking down your nose at people and being snotty to them is only going to result in them taking revenge. This can range from your cleaner doing unmentionable things with your toothbrush to a gynaecologist or plastic surgeon leaking all sorts of personal information. (And on the subject of the former, there's at least one supermodel out there that really needs to learn some manners.)

Waiters

Just because you're forking out a fortune for dinner, don't for one second think you've got the upper hand.

What's really happening is that you're sitting there, helpless, in the hope that they decide to wait on you. Put one foot wrong and they'll all be playing football with your dinner behind closed doors and doing unspeakable things into your wine.

Talking of wine – wine testing just makes you look ridiculous. All that glass swirling and sniffing. If it's just a cheap bottle of plonk or pint of lager then simply smile, say, 'I'm sure it will be perfectly fine,' and you'll let them know if it isn't.

If you've ordered a three-hundred-quid bottle of Château Latour, that's different. Personally, we think it makes you look ridiculously flash to order that stuff, but if you did and it's corked then discreetly whisper to the waiter that things aren't right. Slurping it like a crocodile, shrieking in front of the whole table, yelling 'waiter!' and making a song and dance about it, will leave you looking like even more of an idiot than you did ordering the bottle in the first place. The waiter will respect you for not humiliating the restaurant, treat you with respect and not gargle with your coffee.

Tradesmen

One of the joys of tradesmen is that you get to order them in by phone and they come to your house and do manly things while you watch. Sharon once went through a three-month obsession with a plumber, got the whole bathroom refitted and was seriously considering installing a jacuzzi just to keep him coming.

But that sort of behaviour can get very expensive and it's probably best to steer clear of sex with tradesmen. If they're charging by the hour then take care not to distract them while they're in your home. Either by your behaviour or your clothing. Cover up.

Obviously, don't wear anything really bad like stained velour, as a lady should always look impeccably delicious and clean. But don't bare any flesh or have more than a hint of cleavage. Nothing with holes. Nothing swaying. A nice trouser suit is perfect. High street only, mind. Fabulously cut couture may prove distracting.

Be sweet but authoritative. Remember, they're there to fix things as quickly as possible – not flirt with. (Although that plumber was something!) Don't leave any underwear lying around. Just give them a cup of tea and some firm instructions.

Sleeping with Staff

It is not really appropriate to sleep with staff. But if you get the sudden urge to do a Lady

Chatterley, we understand and we'll let it go just this once. After all, a quick fling doesn't actually count (see page 93).

Go for someone worthwhile, though. For example, the rugged Timberland-type, who chops logs in the forest and will put the smell of the pine in your nostrils, could fit the bill. That sort of thing. Don't have a fling with the milkman in the back of his cart at six in the morning. It's just not chic. Neither's in the red Royal Mail van with the morning post. Believe us, those canvas sacks are a nil threadcount when it comes to comfort.

A good rule of thumb is to work out how important the person is to you. Ask yourself if they are indispensable. How will you feel if you have to fire them afterwards when things don't work out?

If you find a good hairdresser, for example, *never* sleep with him.

Not even if you do get distracted by what's at eye level in their Diesels as they move around to shape your fringe. Good hairdressers are very hard to find. Sharon shares one with Sharon Osborne and wouldn't dream of jeopardising things by offering Lino anything other than a tip.

Be strong. Just pretend you're in Harrods and he's got one of those signs on him saying Do Not Touch. Stick to a blow dry.

Masseurs are fine. There are loads of them.

Tipping

Never mind all those complicated rules on percentages. The basic rule is that the cuter they are and the wider their Colgate smiles, the more cash you give them. If they've been sulky, don't give them anything. Those people that huff and puff like mini dragons every time you ask them to do anything should be sent away empty handed. Or thrown some old lire so it looks like you're giving them loads.

Always tip discreetly. Shake hands with the money in the palm of your hand or pop it in their pocket. No flashing the cash. Don't overtip. Miss TPT has learnt her lesson on that one after going through a phase of picking up beggars in the street who were particularly smiley and nice, checking them into the Four Seasons and getting them dry-cleaned. OK, it felt good to redistribute money to the poor and all that. But as word got out those quick trips to McDonalds got more and more expensive.

If you don't have money on you and it's somewhere you'd really like to return to, improvise. Consider leaving jewellery. Or an old lip gloss. The coat lady at The Shadow Lounge received a worn-down Guerlain lipstick the other day with the assurance that it was a very rare discontinued shade.

Obviously with jewellery go for Swarovski if possible. Tipping with diamonds should only be done if the service was absolutely exceptional.

Please note that it is not necessary/expected to tip medical staff. Unless they have treated a particularly embarrassing condition that you wish them to remain quiet about. Then you should start writing cheques, babycakes. Do note, however, that if you are giving your gynaecologist a cash reward it shouldn't be done in public. You'll only start rumours if you start pulling out the notes in reception.

Be nice to the people who make your life nicer.

The naughty girl needs a good strong team around her and should make sure she keeps them. Do have limits on how nice you are, however. If you have slept with a member of staff it is not necessary to tip them.

PART FOUR:

The Naughty Girl at Home

You've got to get tough with flatmates. **There's absolutely no room for sentiment. If you share and are about to advertise for a new flatmate then make sure you read every word of this chapter. It's crucial to a happy home life.**

PRAYER

Grant me the serenity to recognise that I cannot possibly live with someone who wears paisley underpants

Courage to take full advantage of any amazing skincare products a flatmate leaves unlocked and on display

And the wisdom to ensure I never move anyone in with a better sex life than mine.

The Naughty Girl's Guide to Flatmates

As it's so impossible to get on the mortgage ladder these days, you'll probably spend decades sharing your homespace with flatmates.

Flatmates are strange beings. They're the person you probably spend more time with than anyone else. They sleep metres away from you at night. They'll share your toothpaste. They'll learn everything about you. If we're looking for a lover we do all these tricks like meeting in a public place to check they're not a psycho. Yet with flatmates, you stick an ad up, meet someone for half an hour and then merrily move them into your life and your home.

Here's how to choose one, how to screw everything out of them that you can, and how to cope if it all goes wrong.

God Save the Queen

If at all possible, **then go gay**. Gay is great for flatmates. Let us explain.

✓ *Gay flatmates never let you leave the premises in anything that looks appalling as they'll take it as a personal insult.*
✓ *They take an interest in your clothes and yet never want to borrow them. (Actually they may occasionally try a few things on after a couple of drinks but this is allowed and should be taken as a personal compliment.)*

✓ *They will cheer you off saying things like, 'Go girl. You're looking hot tonight!' And mean it.*

✓ *They are likely to have a fabulous range of cleansers, toners, facemasks, make-up and casual shirts you can steal (see page 181).*

✓ *They happily join in endless bitching about men's shortcomings with you and your girlfriends.*

✓ *They don't mind watching your old eighties Wham! videos.*

✓ *And, if you get a couple of drinks down them and buy them a bag of bananas, they will happily spend the next three hours giving you fantastic tips on your love life.*

✓ *The other bonus of course is that there's absolutely no sexual jealousy whatsoever. If he brings home a man and snogs him on the sofa it will not reinforce the message that you are single and lonely. It will just remind you that you're only single because all men are gay.*
NB: Drag queens are best avoided. They'll only stretch your shoes.

If you insist on going for a female flatmate then don't say we didn't warn you. But do read carefully through this entire chapter before giving anyone the keys to your house.

Placing an Advertisement

When placing your ad for a new person in a newspaper or the Internet, aim to get the maximum number of responses back.

Flat ads are usually soooo dull. They're full of pages about 'light and airy double rooms', demands for 'female n/s' and packed with boring things about kitchens. Make your ad count. Think what your strengths are. Do you know a rugby team? Can you get discounts in any shoe stores? What is your signature dish? Can you mix a decent lychee cocktail? Have you had the house feng shui'd? Are you sleeping with anyone famous? Put that sort of information in. You're selling a lifestyle, not just a room. This will ensure that the maximum number of people apply.

Remember that you are competing for the best potential flatmates available. If photographs are to be used, then invest. Hire a professional film crew if you can afford it. Get one of the makeover companies in to revamp your room with lilies and white furniture. Or, if on a budget, simply retouch the photographs on your computer. Make your towels whiter, maybe remove the wine stains from the carpets. Search on the Internet for pictures of flowers and fabulous home-cooked meals and cut and paste them on to the dining table. Stretch the pictures vertically so it looks like

your ceilings are higher. Don't worry – nobody's house ever looks like it did in the photos. Don't go overboard and start pasting links to Buckingham Palace or Kew Gardens though and start claiming it's yours. There has to be some element of truth. Never put a telephone number as your contact point. Always put your email address in. That way, the person has to respond to the ad by email. You can glean vital information from their email address. If you're lucky it will contain their first name, surname and the name of the company they work for. You can then go off and do a quick Google on them to see if they're members of any weird sex clubs or, worse still, if they work in IT. Type in the whole email address and you'll find out what websites they post to as well. This will give you a quick guide to their interests.

The advantage of email only is that it also helps weed out the types who use 'humorous' nicknames on their email addresses, like 'Ilovehasselfhoff@hotmail.co.uk', or programmingwunderkind@aol.com, or terrywoganrocks@blueyonder.co.uk.

Avoid them like the plague.

NB: Of course this works two ways as they'll have your email address, too. Google yourself. If there's anything dodgy on the Internet about you then set up a new email account using your first name only. Or if you know somebody who leads a fabulous and glamorous lifestyle simply set up an Internet account using their name.

Clothes

Once you're down to your shortlist of fabulous potential new flatmates, arrange for your top choices to come round. Make it evening time so your entire home will be bathed in flattering candlelight and the carpet stains won't be that noticeable.

The point of this meeting is to make a quick assessment of their character, their usefulness to you and the likelihood of you ever catching anything off them if you moved them into your home.

One of the biggest ways of avoiding potential future flatmate grief is to analyse what they are wearing. Clothes are crucial in flatmates. Save yourself a lot of trouble later on by simply watching out of your window or videophone and assessing the potential flatmates as they walk up to your front door. If they're there ringing your doorbell wearing something hideous like paisley or a rainproof poncho then don't even let them in. It'll never work.

Just imagine those clothes hanging on your washing line and then ask if you could really hold your head up in the neighbourhood if people thought they were yours. Just think about what underwear or nightwear they must have if they're prepared to go out like that in public. They probably own a

Viyella dressing gown. Or, even worse, some novelty slippers with floppy ears and noses. Remember, people may think they're yours. Defend your reputation and simply ignore the doorbell.

If they get past the door, then sit them down and have a good stare. Assess. Do you like their clothes?

Don't worry. This isn't being shallow. It's simply being practical.

The question you need to ask is do you want to borrow what they've got on? What are their accessories like? We'll deal with how to nick their stuff on page 181 but now's the time to think what you're likely to be able to get your hands on if you let this person move in.

If they're sitting there in what looks like a much cheaper version of your own outfit, don't even think of letting them move in unless they are at least three dress sizes larger than you. If they're any smaller you run every risk they will want to borrow your fabulous clothes and may even be prepared to diet to get into them.

You will be condemning yourself to evenings cooking huge and fabulous fattening meals and pretending you've 'just eaten' to make sure they stay too fat to get into your stuff.

(NB: If you do end up going for a flatmate who is only slightly fatter, then Charbonnel et Walker make the most fabulous champagne truffles which could also help.)

If their clothes are nicer than yours and you could see yourself going out in them, then give them a big mental tick and move on to the next category. (We deal with how to borrow their fabulous outfits on page 182.)

NB: If they've wandered in wearing couture, they've overdone it. Nobody should wear couture to examine a spare room. Of course, it's possible they've read this book and merely want to make an effort by showing what nice clothes you could nick if only you let them stay. But we say be on your guard. They've probably stolen it. Mainline, diffusion or high street is trustworthier.

> CHECKLIST
> ❑ *Don't be too harsh. Don't reject someone on the basis of a minor transgression like wearing tan tights or last season's heel. Ask yourself if it may be possible to restyle them a little.*
> ❑ *Mohair is a no-no though. It'll only get all over your sofas and lead to endless vacuuming.*

Hygiene

Do check their hygiene. Obviously it is very bad manners to enquire if they've got any STDs at this stage but you can do surface checks to see if there's anything that would make you

reluctant to share a handtowel with this person.

Scan their faces for cold sores. Pretend to admire their lipstick and have a good old stare at their lip line.

As you sit them down, pretend to drop something directly behind them. As you bend to pick it up, have a good scan of their scalp for lice or grease. If they've got a hair ornament use this as an opportunity to linger for a few more seconds examining their locks.

Pretend to admire their jewellery while secretly scrutinising their nails for dirt. If they can't be bothered to scrub their nails it's not likely they'll wash your floors that often either. Having said that – don't necessarily look for a perfect manicure. It's useful to have a flatmate willing to do a bit of scrubbing for you.

Dirty clothes are a no-no, too. If they go out scuffed and stained, then that's how they'll be treating your flat. And think what their underwear must look like. So scan them for evidence of dry-cleaning and steaming.

Obviously it's difficult to get access to the more intimate areas. Maybe hang their coat over the edge of a high door as they come in. That way you'll get a quick discreet scan of their armpits for evidence of shaving and washing as they reach for their coat on the way out.

Looks

We really wouldn't advise going for anyone prettier. Or thinner.

Basically, never ever move anyone in that you are going to get jealous of when you see them in their knickers. You'll just end up depressed if there's a perfect pair of thighs or a lovely retroussé nose down the corridor.

If a vision of loveliness turns up on the doorstep asking to see the flat, then just apply to the paisley rules and don't let them in. Trust us. You don't want the competition. Switch all the lights off and pretend you've gone out until they go away.

What you want is someone who is slightly uglier. Now don't overdo it. You don't want massively ugly. Remember you have to see them first thing in the morning so you don't want someone who frightens you or makes you recoil when you catch them in the mirror. All you're after is someone who isn't quite as fabulous as you are.

The rule of thumb is that if you went out to the Dog and Duck on the pull together, men wouldn't be repelled by your Quasimodo sidekick. But they also wouldn't hesitate to choose you rather than her.

The sort of things that you're looking for are lumpy thighs, mild acne, a spare tyre or maybe a slightly lazy eye. But perhaps not all together. A small twitch can be good, too. You're seeking small design faults so you can still tell your flatmate with a straight face that she 'looks great' while stepping out, confident in the knowledge that you look a lot better.

NB: It helps if they have one major plus point like nice shiny hair. Then you can refer to it constantly and pretend you're jealous so they don't suspect that they've been hired for the role of fat, ugly, deformed flatmate.

Also, don't leave this book around when you're interviewing flatmates. And definitely don't put a large tick next to this chapter as soon as you see them walk through your door. Believe us. That sort of behaviour really upsets people.

Flatmates in Love

Girls, if you've got a man then it's fine for your new flatmate to be in love too. But if you're a singleton it is essential that you only move someone in if you are convinced they aren't getting any action either. The whole point of a flatmate is that you want to feel slightly superior to them.

If you're single never, ever, live with anyone who is in a cosy relationship. Trust us on this one. Living in the middle of *Love Story* is hell. Read our chapter on Smug Marrieds and ask yourself if you really want to live with that full-time.

Of course, if you've got your sex life sorted, then well done you. Skip this chapter, move in with your perfect boyfriend, stop reading us and stop being such a smug cow.

But for the rest of us, the role of a flatmate is to stay single, available and waiting with a bottle of wine to hear all about your problems with the opposite sex and to then console you. It is not to be blissed up and happily in love and to remind you what a failure your own life is.

If at any point you are even thinking about moving in a 'really nice' couple then we urge you to immediately read through this checklist. Ask yourself if you can really live with this sort of s***.

THE COUPLES CHECKLIST

❑ *Every morning when you knock on their door to ask a question, you'll have to stand there for a few awkward seconds while you work out if they're having sex or not. Otherwise you look like a pervert who bangs on their door deliberately during rampant sex sessions. Of course this means it will be down to you to deal with every early morning phone call/postman's knock/tradesman demanding a cup of tea.*

❑ *Every night you will have to wait for them to finish having sex, then have a fag, and finally go to the loo, before you can even think about getting some peace. Throughout the whole thing you will probably hear them giggling together to keep quiet so they won't wake you.*

❏ *You'll have to listen to terribly tedious tales of their holiday excursions. And feign interest at the hundreds of shots of each other on the beach – which were probably taken shortly before having sex.*

❏ *You will come home in the evening to find the living room full of candles and a romantic supper laid out. At this point they will both insist they want you to join them but you know that every fibre in their bodies is willing you to go and sit in your room on your own. Again.*

❏ *Whenever you enter a room, they will do that sudden springing apart thing, and smooth down their clothes as they try to pretend they weren't on the verge of having fabulous sex before you came in and ruined it.*

❏ *When they've finished this fabulous sex they'll feel obliged to spend at least three hours wandering around dressed in inappropriately skimpy towels. Looking smug. And smelling of sweat.*

❏ *They'll look at you in a pitiful way. Especially when you roll in drunk. Alone. At only 9 p.m. Or when you're scowling watching* EastEnders *on your own as they emerge tousled from the bedroom after yet another of their noisy sessions. Some of the worst couples have actually been known to smugly mouth 'Sorry' to the singleton at this point.*

So, in short, avoid. If interviewing a potential new flatmate make it your job to find out straight away if you're likely to have to put up with any of the above.

Don't make it your first question. That's too obvious. Throw it in after, say, making them a cup of tea or showing them the bathroom. Just say, 'So, do you have a partner?' Make it casual.

Nonchalant. Don't even look at them as you say it. Throw it in as if it were a mere afterthought.

Ideal replies are, 'No,' 'No. I once got dumped at the altar and I could never face having another lover.' Or, 'Yes, but he lives abroad/has joined the Foreign Legion/a monastery so we hardly see each other.' If they start pulling out their phone and showing you pictures and gushing, 'Oh yes, here's my little bunny-wunny-woo,' then just tell them that they're such a nice person you have to confess that the room is actually lined with deadly asbestos and you couldn't possibly dream of moving them in.

NB: If they are in love but you still really, really like them, then now is the time to lay down the law. Tell them they can live with you but you don't believe in sex before marriage and they can never, ever bring their lover back to stay. Tell them that it's not that you're a frustrated old hag who's not getting any or anything like that. It's just that it's against your religion. And besides, you read in *Vogue* last week that abstinence was really good for the skin and virginity is the new black in the US.

Flatmate Tests

If there's time, then set a few tests during the interviews.

◆ Have a selection of CDs out on a table. Choose a rave CD, slushy love songs by someone awful like Michael Bolton or James Blunt, a copy of Sinéad O'Connor's 'Nothing Compares 2U', Whitney's 'I Will Always Love You' and then something perfectly normal. Like Kylie. Tell them you're going to make a quick trip to the loo and, hey, could they perhaps stick on a CD for you? Their next move is crucial. If they go for rave, chances are they'll spend their evenings off their face on various drugs and drag their friends back in the early hours. If it's Sinead, they've just been dumped, are still emotionally raw, likely to be pretty high maintenance and want to drunkenly cry on your shoulder every evening. If they go for slush they're clearly in love and are also best avoided (see page 176).

NB: If they pick the normal one then you of course you'll need to backtrack otherwise they'll think you're the one who's a drugged-up deaf depressive. Come in, gasp, 'Oh my God – I didn't mean *that* pile. That's the charity pile I was about to throw out. Look at this rubbish! Glad you managed to find *something* though.'

◆ Leave food, cash, make-up, alcohol, diamond bracelets, a letter marked 'Private and Confidential clinical tests enclosed', a Chloé Paddington bag and perhaps some Prada sunglasses lying temptingly within reach as you leave the room. Memorise the exact position of the objects on the table. Poloraid them if possible. If any are missing or have been moved when you return then you're storing up trouble. If they start trying on your things or sniffing your wine at this early stage then they're going to be ransacking your wardrobe and emptying the fridge the second they move in.

◆ You might also want to drop a bracelet down the loo to see if they nick it or are honest enough to come and tell you that a very expensive diamond family heirloom appears to be nestling in your lavatory pan. (Don't do this with real diamonds unless you're absolutely loaded. A £2.99 cubic zircona piece is perfectly adequate and it won't matter if it's lost in the flush.)

◆ Finally, if there's time, set them a few practical tests. Ask them what their DIY skills are like. Go all Alan Sugar and have some tasks lined up for them to complete to win a place in your home. Maybe hand them a drill and ask them to put up a shelf or two. Perhaps some light painting? If things are going well and it's really clear they want the flat then perhaps go for a spot of grouting in the bathroom. Even if you decide not to let them move in, you could get your entire house revamped if you get through enough interviewees.

Dealing with Unacceptable Flatmate Behaviour

Don't think your problems are over once your flatmate has moved in. Bear in mind that during their first month, any flatmate will be red-hot on household tasks. You're in that honeymoon period where you're offering to cook for each other, spending evenings chatting over a bottle of wine and practically fighting to wash up.

Of course, none of this will last. Within a few short weeks you'll be leaving stroppy Post-its to each other and bitching about them and their cleaning rotas to your workmates. This is perfectly normal behaviour and you shouldn't worry about it. But there are certain things which are unacceptable and should be spotted early, and immediately dealt with.

If possible, get your flatmate to sign on for a three-month trial period, after which they're out in the event of a breakdown. Otherwise, here's how to nip those little problems in the bud:

PROBLEM: THEY WANT TO BORROW YOUR CLOTHES.
Hopefully you will have avoided this by getting in a flatmate who

is much fatter than you (see page 165). If not, and she starts making noises about wanting to borrow your clothes for big occasions, then fret not. There is still a way round it.

You must be ruthless from day one. Go out and buy two sets of a fabulous new outfit. One in your size. The other two sizes smaller. Come home, show off your lovely new outfit, then tell her she simply must try it on too. Go into the bedroom and swap it for the smaller version. Give her that version to try on. She will strain and squeeze and eventually drag it over her thighs. Wince a lot and make noises like, 'Be careful not to tear it.' Once on, it will, of course, look awful.

Trust us. She will never borrow that outfit. In fact, she will never borrow ANY of your outfits. She will be far too mortified from realising how much fatter than you she is and that she very nearly split the seams of your new clothes.

Having said that, we're not aiming to give anyone a weight complex here – just to keep their hands off your clothes. So hand them dignity in defeat. The best thing to do is to look at them and say something like, 'Of course, that dress is designed for flat-chested people like me. I wish I had your curves, you know. You're so voluptuous. You should be sharing with Kelly Brook. It's not fair. I'm not even going to try to put on your clothes – I'll just end up depressed and wanting surgery.' For added effect you can make sure they catch you Googling 'breast enhancement' and sighing heavily later on that evening.

You could also pop into your room and come back with something that you don't mind lending, like a pair of sunglasses or a scarf, and go into raptures about how amazing they look in it.

Mind you, if she still persists in wanting to borrow your best clothes, it's time to get tough. Just mutter darkly that clearly you've got such different figures. Say, 'Remember we tried with that outfit that time . . .' Then trail off and stare pointedly at her thighs.

NB: Of course, once you've done this clothes-swapping trick you simply take the smaller version of the outfit back to the shop for a full refund.

PROBLEM: THEY SNOOP IN YOUR ROOM.
You'll find out what your flatmate is really like when you go away for the weekend. This is her golden opportunity to snoop around your stuff, safe in the knowledge that she can dress up in your clothes, romp in your bed, try out your make-up and borrow all your bags and still have forty-eight hours to make any necessary repairs or replacements.

So be aware and prepare.

If you've got the budget, then CCTV in your room is always good. If not Polaroid everything. Open your wardrobe and get a picture of exactly how everything is positioned within. Mark tiny lines on your bath oil and face creams. Have a record of the exact angle your handbags, shoes and sunglasses were lying at when you left the room. That way you'll know what's been moved.

Be realistic. There's nothing wrong with a five-minute snoop through your stuff. This is the perk of having a flatmate. So let her have just a little look through. Your goal is to ensure that she doesn't get to any of the interesting stuff or borrow your better clothes. The purpose of the CCTV or Polaroids is simply to give you some ammunition should she discover that you've been regularly going through her stuff and wearing her clothes. You could also leave some cash lying around. The CCTV cameras will show if the little thief is nicking it, or if it really is the cleaner as she's been claiming for the past few weeks.

If you suspect a snooping flatmate and you're going away, it's a good idea to leave a few tempting decoys on the bed – a couple of outfits you hate, and perhaps some accessories as well. You then write her a note suggesting which of her shoes and handbags would coordinate best with these items to make you look generous and thoughtful. Another advantage of doing this is that it will discourage your flatmate from sleeping in your bed for the night, or drunkenly inviting her friends to crash there. They will know that they are unlikely to be able to exactly recreate the arrangement on the bed and will therefore have to confess someone's slept in it and have to go through the bother of washing and drying all your sheets.

Leave a couple of bank statements out on the bed so they can have a nosey through them, sate their curiosity and hopefully not go through the rest of your private paperwork or diaries.

Before you set off, work out what you don't want them to touch, see or borrow. Cover your best items with dry-cleaning bags and place right at the back of the wardrobe. Nobody will risk tearing off the plastic covers as they won't have time to track down the dry-cleaners and get the item cleaned, bagged and replaced before your return.

Leave out tubes of half-used verruca cream or wart removal gels. These should ensure your shoes are not worn. Canesten cream will guarantee your skinny jeans and best underwear are left untouched.

Put all personal stuff like diaries, your best jewellery or favourite hat into one drawer. Put a huge sex toy on the top of it all. Trust us, there's no way they'll move one of those and go ferreting through the stuff underneath it. If you've got a favourite handbag you don't want them to borrow then simply put the large sex toy in that as well. Not only will they put it back hastily, but you can have hours of fun later by refusing to tell them where you're going on a night out and making sure you're carrying that particular handbag.

If you've got a favourite pair of shoes or dress or bath oil you don't want them to borrow or try on under any circumstances, then just simply take it with you. It may seem odd packing Jimmy Choos or a ballgown for a hiking trip but it's better to be safe than sorry.

Hide your car keys too.

PROBLEM: THEY'RE ON DRUGS.
This is bad. You don't want to share your life with this person. Simply leave some soap powder laid out in a neat white line on the kitchen table before retiring to bed at night. If you wake up the next morning to find them dead, with blood pouring from their nose or with exceptionally soapy nostrils, then, yes, they were on drugs. But the good news is you've dealt with it now.

NB: Oh, OK. We've just had a note from the lawyers. They say that killing people is against the law. So maybe just talcum powder. Or book them into The Priory.

PROBLEM: THEY KEEP GOSSIPING ABOUT YOU.

It's not really a problem, is it? **Naughty girls are bound to get gossiped about** because their life is so much more interesting than their flatmate's. Just give them something good to gossip about. Tell them you're having a mad affair with Brad Pitt and sit back and see if you're on the front page of the *Sun* the next morning.

PROBLEM: THEY KEEP LEAVING THEIR OLD GREY KNICKERS AND BRAS HANGING AROUND.
A lesser crime – but still one that needs instant action. After all, people may think they're yours. Keep a beady eye out for the next

time the offending items are put into the wash. Then simply pop home at lunchtime, shove in your black cashmere sock and stick on the wash cycle again. It'll 'accidentally' dye the whole lot black and you can claim they must have failed to spot the sock when they loaded up the machine.

PROBLEM: THEY'RE HAVING ENDLESS SEX.
Ah. This is the biggie. You clearly weren't paying attention when we advised you how to stop yourself living in the middle of *Love Story*, were you?

Never mind. It's not too late. We can still help.

If you're spending every night lying awake until 2 a.m., waiting for their bedsprings to shut up, then it's time to take action. Be ruthless. If it's wild, rampant noisy and non-stop and includes howling through the walls then, girl, just face it, they are showing absolutely nil respect for you, so don't show them a scrap of mercy.

NB: Do make sure all their bills are up to date and paid before trying any of this. These techniques are quite extreme and they'll probably pack their bags and leave. Oh, and don't get carried away and do everything on this list. You'll get arrested. Subtlety is everything. Just pick your favourite one or two.

◆ First try being nice for a week. Try feng shui. This dictates that anything placed in pairs – like shoes – will lead to a happy coupling. So go through their room and subtly move each pair of shoes one inch apart. Water symbols and colours can dampen their ardour, too. Buy them a lovely set of blue bedsheets. Or a waterbed.

Give that seven days then start getting evil. We've had to deal with this sort of thing a lot so we've got plenty of suggestions. Sharon had one couple who actually held hands during dinner. Yuk.

◆ Remember there's strength in numbers. If it's the two of them against you, you can end up feeling outnumbered and intimidated. They'll be utterly wrapped up in their passion and won't give a toss about you and the misery they're causing. So get your friends in. Sit in your room and eat pizza. Tara recommends Waitrose's cheese fondue. Then wait until the end of their next sex marathon and erupt into cheers and whoops, holler and applaud wildly through the walls. If you have the time to prepare, pile into the room brandishing scorecards and award points for artistic interpretation as well. Ask if you could all stay and watch.

◆ Put up a narrow shelf, slightly at an angle, on the other side of their wall outside their bedroom. Balance lots of glass vases on it. Their wall-shaking and pounding will be constantly interrupted by the sound of vases smashing one by one on the floor. If possible, fill them all with lilies. Old lily water reeks so this will have the added bonus of creating a stink just outside their love palace, leading to a peaceful interlude as they struggle with the bleach and carpet freshener.

◆ If your budget runs to it, you could arrange for a full firework display complete with Elgar's *Land of Hope and Glory* and Handel's *Music for the Royal Fireworks* to be performed outside their window. If you can't afford the London Philharmonic, a good CD played at full volume could work almost as well. That should do the trick.

◆ Try dampening their sex drive by putting them off each other. Leave large tubes of Vagisil and Anusol in the bathroom. In case they think they're yours, ask, 'Who on earth do these belong to?'

◆ Every week steal at least one condom from her room (the box is usually kept in the top bedside drawer). Eventually they'll notice the numbers going down and grow horribly suspicious of each other. You should also help yourself to a good pour of their massage oil each week. They'll notice the bottle slowly emptying and start suspecting each other.

◆ You could also steal her best knickers and put them under the bed, as if they had been flung there in a moment of rampant passion. Rumple the sheets a little too.

◆ If she goes out to the gym, pop in to see him and say you're just returning the magazines she lent you. He's bound to flick through. Make the second one down a bridal magazine. For added points, circle several of the dress designs inside. And have copies of her signature with his surname written twenty times on the cover. With luck, he'll pack and leave before she's even finished her warm-ups.

◆ If either of them approach you and accuse you of doing any of this stuff look them straight in the eye, blame the other and say, 'Hey! Just keep me out of your private rows. I don't want to know. Of course I didn't do it. What sort of sick puppy do you think I am? I've never been so insulted in my life. (Pause before raising your voice and shouting.) Now get out of my life and get out of my flat!'

Don't feel guilty. Remember it's their fault in the first place for having a fabulous sex life, rubbing your nose in it, and not having the decency to take their blatant love life elsewhere. Such as his flat.

IF ALL ELSE FAILS, JUST SLEEP WITH HIM YOURSELF. She'll soon move out in a huff.

What is Acceptable Behaviour from You?

The trick is to make your flatmate toe the line, while getting away with absolute murder yourself. They should be the nice flatmate. You're the naughty one.

Provided you know exactly how to do it, you can regularly snoop round their room, borrow their clothes and nick their skincare. It's all about technique.

SNOOPING

You should be assessing their room regularly and having a good look around to see what's new that's worth borrowing.

For short snooping sessions while your flatmate is out it's essential to arm yourself with a cover story. Bring the washing in for them. That will buy yourself a good five minutes in their room as you carefully fold each item in a neat pile on their bed. If they catch you and question you, act hurt and affronted and tell them they can do their own darned household chores from now on.

SKINCARE

If you are sharing with someone who happens to have great skin, then it is only natural you will want to find out what their secret is. And try it out for yourself. The trick here is to ration your 'borrowing'. If you're mainlining her Eve Lom she's going to notice. Take a tiny sample and she'll never know. It's maths time again.

THE MATHS

To remain undetected please limit skincare thieving to the following:

Facial wash: One pump per week.

Moisturiser: One sample the size of a twenty-pence piece every two days.

Bath oil: Three baths a month.

Face mask: One mask per month.

Crème de la Mer: Be fair. This stuff costs a fortune. One application every three months. Oh, go on then, perhaps two.

Body scrubs: Use as much as you like. Simply top it up with rock salt once you've finished. (NB: Ordinary kitchen salt doesn't work.)

Face exfoliants: As above. Just shove in some sand.

Nail varnish: Natural French manicure can be reapplied on a weekly basis – especially the white, as white never runs out. Dark colours should only be used on toenails during winter as she's bound to notice you wearing it otherwise.

Of course, if your flatmate is going away for a few days you can have all sorts of fun. This is a golden opportunity to borrow her handbag, hold fabulous dinner parties in her best outfits and have a good rummage round her family-heirloom jewellery. Just make sure you do the following:

✓ *Polaroid the room before borrowing anything or take a picture using your mobile phone. That way you can ensure you replace everything exactly where you found it.*

✓ *Avoid making any TV appearances or being photographed wearing anything of hers.*

✓ *Think where you are going. Will the outfit smell when you get back? If you're planning on wearing it to a sweaty club/curry-eating competition/bonfire night then this will be a giveaway. We're not saying don't borrow it. Just ensure you factor in enough time to leave it hanging on the line outside for a night to get rid of the smells.*

✓ *Only wear their jewellery while in the safety of your own home. If you lose it when you're out you'll have to go through the time, stress and insurance nightmare of faking a raid on your home.*

✓ *Take care with shoes. If they are in light, delicate, stainable colours, don't risk going out in them. Suede is an absolute no-no. Restrict those to home cocktail parties only. If the shoes are snakeskin then go ahead and dance all night in them. They never stain. New shoes are also best avoided as you'll end up with an outline of your feet in them. Also remember that new shoes give you blisters. So only go for ones that she has already broken in for you.*

✓ *If they're stupid enough to leave the car keys then feel free to borrow it. Take it and enjoy it here, there and everywhere and have a good party. Just get it valeted when you're through. On the day she arrives back, smile sweetly and say, 'Do you know what? I've missed you so much I got your car cleaned for you.' She'll be so grateful. NB: Always pay the Congestion Charge and take care not to speed. The little b***ards enclose photos now and it would be bad to have a snapshot of you driving around in her car, wearing all her best clothes.*

✗ *It is unacceptable to break open any locks to get to skincare items or nice pieces of jewellery. If they've made*

the effort to lock them away you should respect that.
Remember you're naughty. Not wicked.

✗ *Borrowing their boyfriend is also bad. Unless, as we've*
said, you want to split them up.

Choose your flatmate badly and you'll be condemning yourself to a homelife of utter misery watching somebody much thinner than you snogging on the sofa, while all the time you could have had blemish-free skin and a fabulous wardrobe all at their expense. So don't worry if any of this advice seems harsh – it's just that being naughty will make your experience so much nicer.

In short, girls, your ideal flatmate is rich, gay, drug-free, wears fabulous clothes, has amazing jewellery, a great car, loves Kylie, has access to gorgeous single men and spends a fortune on pampering themselves.

Basically, you're looking for the closest thing to Elton John you can find.

PART FIVE:

The Naughty Girl's Guide to Money

PRAYER

*Grant me the serenity to accept my salary may not
extend to couture*

Courage to go own-brand in times of trouble

*And the wisdom to always look a million dollars,
even if that's the amount I owe.*

The Naughty Girl's Guide to Being Strapped for Cash

Everyone's strapped for cash sometimes. It's no excuse to let standards slip. Incidentally, if you're really broke and you still bought our book then thank you. Like we said at the start, if you borrowed it from the library, it's the thought that counts. And if it's borrowed from a friend that's OK too. If she's looking great she's obviously read it already and doesn't need it any more. If she looks terrible then she clearly hasn't bothered paying any attention to us. It's high time you had a go instead.

Now then, we're sure you're perfectly capable of working out all the boring stuff about going for walks in parks, visiting free outdoor concerts, cooking pasta and buying economy brands to save cash.

So we'll leave the duller books to patronise you with all that. Here's our guide on how to look fabulous, blag freebies, and throw amazing parties, so you'll look like you're loaded even when you're not.

Immediate Help

Our three top tips are sofas, couture outlets and old people. For more get-rich-quick ideas see page 199.

SOFAS

You may well already be sitting on a fortune. The average sofa is usually carrying enough cash for at least a main course at The Ivy. Every time a bloke sits on one, all the loose change rolls merrily out of his pocket and down the space at the back.

So, if you're skint, the trick is to visit as many sofas as possible.

Start with your own sofa. Turn over all the cushions and have a good root down the back. Every time you have a male guest ensure he sits in the seat that has the squishiest cushion to ensure he sinks as far back as possible. As soon as he leaves check to see what gifts he may have left behind.

Visit other people's sofas. Go round to houses that you know are full of men. Apply for job interviews you don't really want. Ride on buses. Go on daytime TV shows. Basically think of sofa opportunities and go for them. As soon as you're on the sofa then, as discreetly as you can, shove your hand down the back and have a ferret around. If caught, claim to have dropped something, like a ring, to give yourself an excuse to strip it bare and pocket the cash.

You could spend an extremely profitable afternoon by visiting sofa showrooms like World of Leather or DFS. Hundreds of cash-carrying men will have tried out those sofas and there could be rich pickings. Especially during the sales. Kingcome Sofas on the Fulham road and Harrods' soft furnishings department are also possible sources of loose change, but don't be disappointed if the latter only throws up foreign coins.

COUTURE

Just because you're on a cut-price budget doesn't mean you can't wear couture.

Unless you're an impoverished celeb or supermodel, it's unlikely you'll be able to borrow an entire outfit. But anyone

can get their hands on a couture carrier bag which is an invaluable tool for bluffing.

Dress in your most stylish outfit and then simply pop into somewhere like Chanel and tell them that you're a stylist doing a photo shoot up the road. Ask if you could possibly have one of their carrier bags just for the model to hold.

Keep hold of this bag. Take this bag with you wherever you go as people will assume you've just dropped a fortune in Chanel, are utterly loaded and they will fawn all over you. You can also leave it casually lying about your flat. When guests arrive, they'll think they've caught you post-couture-spending.

If you have any rich relatives or friends you can use the bag to hand over a cheap gift like costume jewellery. Simply present it in the bag and the grateful recipient will think you've spent a fortune and feel obliged to buy you madly expensive gifts in return.

Do bear in mind that you should only use this trick when the bag is in pristine condition. If you keep carrying it around when it's dog-eared they'll know you're faking it.

OLD PEOPLE

Old people are fabulous. Never ignore them. They made it through fourteen years of rationing, remember. They can help you through the odd rough patch. They are an often overlooked source of advice, cooking tips and knitting skills. So we say be really adorable to every old person, always. Hip replacement is hip. Forget Chloé bags. Colostomy bags are in.

You should always be on the lookout for old people who wear expensive jewellery. At the first sight of pearls you should be out there like a whippet helping them across roads, doing their shopping, visiting them and that sort of thing. Remember – if there's jewellery on the OAP go OTT. You never know, they just might remember you in their will.

(Incidentally, if you're an elderly person who's strapped for cash, simply hang around wearing expensive jewellery and keep mentioning that you're really ill. Tell people that you're off to your solicitors soon to alter your will. You should find that people fall over themselves to help you.)

Throwing a Party

If you're broke, the trick is to try and live off the generosity of others. You should aim to accept as many invitations as possible so you can eat and drink your way through other people's fridges before going back to your own empty one.

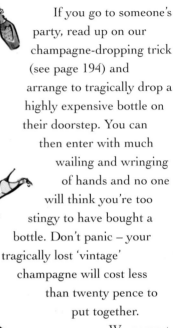

If you go to someone's party, read up on our champagne-dropping trick (see page 194) and arrange to tragically drop a highly expensive bottle on their doorstep. You can then enter with much wailing and wringing of hands and no one will think you're too stingy to have bought a bottle. Don't panic – your tragically lost 'vintage' champagne will cost less than twenty pence to put together.

We suggest that you wait for your birthday and throw a huge party. This is the perfect opportunity to attract a mountain of gifts. You can then eBay the presents afterwards. Even if your funds are small you should always think big. If you invite a hundred people that's you sorted dinner-wise for the next three months.

Here's how to throw a party for a hundred for twenty-five pounds. Yes, we know it sounds less likely than the picnic in the Bible where they feed five thousand with just two fish and five loaves. But it is possible. And it can include your outfit.

THE OUTFIT

You may be strapped for cash but never let things slip appearance-wise. Nails clean, hair washed, make-up professionally applied (for free of course, see page 192). You should look fabulously well maintained. **Image is everything.**

Next, go out and buy an amazing outfit. (Don't worry if it's over budget. All you have to do is check that you can return the outfit – for a full refund – to the shop. Tell them you just want to go home and check it will match your shoes.) This fabulously expensive outfit is now yours (temporarily, anyway) to greet your guests at the party.

However there is a limit. Girls, you must only wear the borrowed clothes for the FIRST HOUR of the evening. This is the longest as you can reasonably get away with wearing a dress and still be able to return it 'unworn' to the shop the next day.

Be careful not to sit down in it as this will cause tell-tale creases. You shouldn't smoke in it or allow any other smokers near you. And you MUST powder your pits before you put it on. BO is a no-no when returning. And do not even think about red wine. Then, having posed for lovely photographs with all your guests so that your fabulously expensive outfit is recorded for eternity, announce that you're off to your bedroom to 'slip into something more comfortable'.

Hang up the outfit in front of an open window and it can then be returned as good as new the next day. (NB: Do not spray it with Febreze. Anyone can spot that sickly-sweet smell a mile off and shop assistants will know immediately what's been going on. If the outfit reeks then hang it on the washing line until it doesn't.)

Now you've made your big entrance and taken photos, it doesn't matter what you wear for the rest of the party. Tracksuits or plain silk pyjamas are both perfectly OK and you can pretend that arriving in your old joggers or nightwear is just a humorous twist on the exotic meet-and-greet outfit.

YOUR MAKE-UP

If you go to one make-up counter and ask them to do an entire makeover, the assistants will get stroppy and try to brow beat you into buying a lipstick or something. The trick is to spread your freebie make-up raid across several stores as some of these people have a mean trick of just doing half your face, to show you the before and after.

So, on the day of your party pop along to one store and ask for help with your foundation and concealer. After they've applied it for you, say you've got sensitive skin and you want to check you don't have a reaction to it before buying. Thank them and leave.

Then simply move from store to store. Go to one for help with eyeshadow, another for tips with cheeks, down the road for luscious lips. Don't forget one final store to set the lot with face powder so it lasts until your party.

If you've got time, and a big enough list of shops, you could actually get a cleanse, tone and moisturising treatment and possibly even a face pack using this method. And it doesn't hurt to ask for samples either as they make invaluable thank you gifts (see page 196).

Last stop is the scent counter. Sample a generous spray of your favourite on the pulse points and other extremities, then head home. Pop on your borrowed outfit, taking care not to smudge your borrowed make-up, and you're good to go.

THE DRINKS

Write on your invitation that 'there will be a limited free bar but guests are also invited to bring their own bottles'. Don't be embarrassed. People in very grand houses regularly ask guests to bring a bottle (although the friend who took along some Jacob's Creek to Buckingham Palace did have it discreetly taken from him at the door).

Personally, we think it's bloody rude of anyone to turn up at your party without some sort of offering. You're providing your fabulous couture-clad company. The least they can do is fork out a tenner on some booze.

Don't let anyone in who breaks this rule. Watch on the intercom or from the window to see if they are carrying any likely presents. If you can't quite see then ask them to step back a bit and pretend to be admiring their outfits or manicures so you can scan them and check they've bought gifts. If they're empty-handed say cheerily, 'Oh (insert name) was looking for you. Something urgent. She's just gone to Threshers – why not see if you can catch up with her?' Again, this may sound a bit strict but remember, you're skint – this is no time for charity.

Now for the drinks. Budget around fifteen pounds for this. You need a large bottle of Appletiser or Babycham, one good bottle of red, and one of those boxes of white wine that last for ever.

A week before your party, go round some expensive restaurants and ask if you can have any empty champagne or wine bottles. Tell them it's for an art project. The more expensive the brand the better. Good names to look for are Krug and Château Latour.

Before your guests arrive, decant the fizzy apple juice into the empty champagne bottles. Then pour the wine from the box into the empty (washed) expensive wine bottles. Cork and chill. Decant the decent bottle of red between five or six empty bottles so you've got what looks like six wildly expensive bottles of wine with just one glass of wine left in each. Keep this in the kitchen as an all-night prop.

Next up, it's time to greet your guests. Work out which of your male guests are the richest and the most generous. Give them an arrival time an hour earlier than anyone else to make sure they arrive first. Hopefully they'll be bearing gifts of the alcoholic type, as requested on the invitation, which you will graciously and gratefully accept. Sit them on the sofa (see page 187) and pop into the kitchen to 'fix them all some fabulously expensive champagne cocktails'.

Shut the kitchen door behind you, give it a minute, then throw all the champagne bottles onto the floor so they explode with an almighty crash. Scream. (NB: Make sure it's a hard floor, if it's carpet they'll just bounce. You may wish to practise with a couple of bottles before to check the exact force needed for the best effects and shattered glass.) As your male guests rush in, floods of tears are de rigueur as you gulp that you've just tripped up and sent the whole lot crashing. Blame the dog if you have one. If you can't summon tears on the spur of the moment, apply a little menthol lip balm like Carmex (see page 86) to your eyes just before you pull this stunt. This will make your eyes stream. Make sure your mascara is waterproof.

They will see what appears to be hundreds of pounds' worth of champagne oozing across the floor, you sobbing away in an absolute state, saying you can't believe this has happened and what on earth are you going to do now as you have no champagne to serve your guests. At this stage the men should immediately offer to do the decent thing and rush out to buy you replacement bottles. With luck they'll make it vintage, as they'll be far too embarrassed to fob you off with a replacement Cava when you'd clearly spent a fortune on Krug.

(NB: We recommend Appeltiser for this trick as it's the right colour and also has the right amount of fizz and is used all the time on film sets to stop actors getting drunk when filming champagne scenes. Old bottles of Babycham would also do the trick. Anything with an obvious aroma, like lager, will be a giveaway if they come in and the kitchen smells like a brewery.)

This sorts out the champagne. As for the wine, you should be covered as the guests start to bring their own contributions. Keep up appearances by pouring your cheap box into the expensive bottles that are dotted about the house to create the illusion that they've all been drinking through your fabulously classy wine collection.

Even if any wine snobs do realise that the wine doesn't taste quite as fabulous as it ought to, they should be polite enough not to comment, especially as you've already seen a case of luxurious champagne ruined. If they do make any negative remarks smile pointedly and ask if they've brought any bottles of their own vastly superior wine choice that you can offer instead. Then direct them to the local off-licence.

FLORAL DISPLAYS

Floral displays are essential in creating the right atmosphere.

Turn to God. Frequent your local church.

Churches tend to have fresh flowers for Sunday services so it should be easy to persuade a nice vicar or the parishioner in charge to give you the old ones on Saturday.

Alternatively, if a TV show is being filmed near you then work out on which day it is and then scour the bins outside for flowers. They nearly always throw away heaps of beautiful fresh flowers from the set. Likewise, posh parties or magazine shoots.

As we've said before, taking flowers from hospitals is forbidden. Even if they're in a coma and won't even notice. That's being bad. It's better to go without.

MAGAZINES

Magazines always look good dotted around. These can be 'borrowed' from dentists' and doctors' waiting rooms, and beauty salons. Again, we ask you not to take them from a hospital, please.

THE CATERING

If you've made friends with old ladies like we suggested (see page 189) catering will not be a problem. This is the bit where the grannies come into their own. They are wonderful beings who used to feed entire families on one dried-egg coupon during the war.

They always have cupboards of basics from which they can magic up fresh loaves, cupcakes and biscuits. If you give them a tenner they'll be able to add in a nice nutritious warming stew and a good solid buffet.

The next day you simply take round the flowers as your thank you. Plus, any of the presents you've been given that you think would look nice in their home. If they did a particularly fabulous job give them all your make-up counter skincare samples. Present them in the Chanel bag for added effect.

Remember, it's ladies in their golden years that have the Midas touch. Play your cards right and you may even be able to convince them to knit your entire party outfit for you.

If you haven't been helping the aged, you're on your own. Don't worry. We'll help.

(Incidentally, if you're an old person reading this book, demand an invitation to the party and say you want at least twenty pounds. You could even set up a catering business to help useless young women, which will support you throughout your retirement.)

HORS D'OEUVRES

Two days before the party start visiting all the food departments of your local stores, markets and supermarkets. Take a doggy bag and help yourself to any free food samples you can find. Go several times during the day as they tend to change the samples by the hour.

Wear hats, scarves and veils to disguise yourself if you're returning many times during the course of the day. If you know someone who might lend you a hijab, this is a bonus as you can then get in there every ten minutes. Plus, they look a lot more attractive than a balaclava.

If you're in London, try Borough Market for food freebies. Harrods has a brilliant food hall, as does Selfridges.

You should be able to get all manner of things from the smarter stores if you say you're planning a massive catering event and would like to try some samples. Go shopping with a massive trolley as if you're planning to buy loads of things. Take your Chanel bag with you and casually wave it about to look as if spending a load of

money in designer shops is second nature to you. Buy one sample and ask for a carrier bag or box.

These samples are your hors d'oeuvres. Even if you've only managed to collect a couple of mouthfuls, it's enough. Hide them and then bring in the plate halfway through the party, looking a bit flustered, and give the remains to the richest person in the room gasping, 'God, these are going down soooo well in the other room. Here, I saved you a couple. There were loads more but the others were on me like gannets.'

After that, if you don't have an old ladies' buffet to support you, the easiest thing to do is spend the rest of your cash on chips.

Nobody is ever too posh for chips.

Present them in an amusing way – like in your Harrods or Chanel carrier bag – and they will be a fabulous talking point.

CHECKLIST

❑ *When begging for discounts, use your imagination. Take supermarkets, for instance. Everybody just mopes around with their trolleys on automatic pilot, picking up their food and asking the store staff where the loo rolls live. Have you considered staging a formation dancing display with your trolley in front of the fish counter? What about performing a specially written verse asking for thirty per cent off some skate? At the very least they should give you a darned good tip-off about what time they'll be moving stuff over to the discount section.*

❑ *Don't be too shy to ask for donations but it's easier if your friends think they're helping make history rather than helping you to sponge off them. Pile every last coin you have into a massive tower in the living room. Invite rich friends and, when they ask why you've built a mountain of pound coins, tell them that you're hoping to enter the 'Guinness Book of Records' for the largest pile and only need five more. They're bound to look in their purse. Pretend to get excited and take pictures of them standing next to the world record they helped to create.*

❑ *You can also lie through your teeth and tell those of your friends that cook that the party is a giant 'who can bring the best canapés' competition. They'll come laden with exotic trays. If any of them question you about judges or prizes, simply burst into Carmex tears and say the prize was to have been a bottle of vintage champagne.*

❑ *Pose as a journalist. Scan your local newspaper for incredibly dull exhibitions, poetry recitals or obscure computer chipset launches that no self-respecting journalist would turn up to. Go along and claim you're writing for something incredibly important like* Tatler, Vogue *or the* Sunday Sport. *You'll be led to the free bar and fawned over all evening. Dress for the part, though. Don't go in a stained tracksuit if you're pretending to work for* Vogue, *and don't turn up clutching* Heat *magazine and claim you're with the* Economist. *And don't get hammered on the free bar unless you're claiming to work for one of the tabloids. Remember, you're not lying. You will be reporting on the event for the publication – the fact that the publication is likely to reject the piece as it's never heard of you is beside the point. Do try and remember to ask a couple of intelligent questions. (Or ask for bust sizes if you're allegedly from the* Sport.)*

❑ *Are you making full use of any local celebrities? Carol-singing is always an excellent ploy. If you've got a celebrity who lives close to you then simply stand outside their home at Christmas time, take sweet children, then ring the doorbell and work your way through a couple of carols. Have a friend parked nearby taking lots of pictures through their front window. The celebrity will spot them, panic that it's for a tabloid newspaper article like, 'How generous are celebrities to Christmas carol-singers?' and dig deep.*

❑ *You could also double your money by actually flogging the pictures of the incredibly generous celebrities to the* Sun.

❑ *Adapt your wardrobe. Look at celebs' feet. You will notice they all have red-soled shoes as they wear fabulously expensive Louboutins. Grab some red paint or nail varnish and adapt your soles to match.*

❑ *If you have any designer clothes then unpick the label and simply transfer it into the item of clothing you are wearing that day. If anyone spills something down you or burns a cigarette through it, here is a golden opportunity to raise some more cash. Accept no less than fifty pounds for 'specialist dry-cleaning' and up to four hundred if the person appears quite drunk, gullible or you don't like them very much. Remember, you are not being a cow. They have just ruined your vintage dress.*

Listen, if the old budget doesn't quite stretch to couture then don't despair. Whether your budget screams Armani or Asda, you should still get out there and party.

Just because your bank account is empty doesn't mean your diary ever should be.

There is nothing shameful in being poor. The landed gentry may be land rich but they're cash poor thanks to generations of gambling and/or debauchery. You're in very good company, believe us.

Skint is chic.

PART SIX:

The Naughty Girl Abroad

Right. Now, we hope you bought a decent bikini (see page 125 for buying tips). And that you needed valium because your waxing session was so thorough. All sorted? OK. Now we'll deal with how to have a good time abroad.

PRAYER

Grant me the serenity not to get depressed at the thought of being in public in swimwear

Courage to pull the best-looking man on the beach

And the wisdom to know that even if I do have cellulite, I'm still a goddess.

The Naughty Girl's Guide to Travelling as a Singleton

Picking a Holiday Companion

This is all pretty similar to the flatmate suggestions (see chapter four). You're looking for someone who's just that bit uglier and fatter than you. Not so much that you're going to get lost in the lard when men scour the beach for someone to talk to. Just someone slightly worse off than yourself so men will be automatically drawn to admire you. If all your friends are fabulously good-looking, don't worry. Just search the beach when you get there and always park yourself next to someone much larger and plainer than yourself.

How to Look Alluring on a Beach

You're single. So we presume you're after holiday romance. Just remember at breakfast time that you're intending to spend the rest day wearing just your bra and pants while trying to attract the opposite sex. So don't go bloating yourself up with a mountains of croissants, loads of bread and a full fry-up. Save the big meals for the evening when you can hide things under a restaurant table and you're wearing more material.

Now then, you may be on holiday but day one is no time to relax. Your first appearance on the beach or sun lounger is crucial.

This is the only time when it is acceptable to go over in your knickers and bra to a strange man and ask him to massage you.

If you're a single girl then this is the moment the boys will be seeing you for the first time. The men will be checking out how your butt compares to everyone else's. So follow our checklist.

CHECKLIST

❑ *While walking to your sunbathing spot you need to suck that tummy in. Don't worry. This isn't permanent and you can let it all hang out in a minute. It's just for the initial stroll along the beach. Think catwalk. Remember that you will be getting checked out for the first time. So don't let that belly sag, don't smoke a fag and don't have a row down the mobile with someone. Saunter down the beach looking hot to trot with your chest pushed out.*

❑ *If your bottom and thighs do not exactly have supermodel proportions then we suggest a spot of subterfuge. Burrow a little ditch in the sand. Place your towel over the dip and lie in the shallow. From the side your behind will then look at least two dress sizes smaller. If you're on a sunbed you can create the same effect by artfully arranging a towel around your thighs.*

❑ *Unless you've paid for them or they're naturally pert, we say don't go topless. Leave something to the imagination. Men like the challenge of undressing you. And besides, if you've got a top on, you can pad out, wire up, lift and separate and look so much better than you do naked.*

❑ *Beaches are a nightmare to look elegant on. The sand blows and sticks to your sun lotion. It's impossible to apply cream to your bottom in public without looking ridiculous. You look hot, you look sweaty and you look stupid as you try and rub that thick smear of white sun lotion into your face.*

❑ *So, for maximum appeal it's best to prepare before you leave the hotel room. Do the whole suncream application thing in the bathroom before you leave so you can go through a nice sexy top-up routine when you arrive on the beach. Sexily stroke a little oil into your arms like they do on those suncream ads and avoid all that rubbing under the udders in public.*

❏ *Every hour or so pop back to your hotel to reapply lotion, perhaps change your bikini or put on some more waterproof mascara. This enables you to check there's no male talent further down the beach that you are missing out on and also to get out of the sun and check you're not turning red. Remember, holidays are for eating lobster. Not looking like one.*

Applying Back Cream

Single girls can use suncream application as a valuable pulling tool. If you're out on the beach with a girlfriend and there are any nice men nearby, you should work in tandem. One of you should go and buy some water so the other can embark on the tried-and-tested 'my back is burning' routine.

You should start applying suncream and seductively stroke it over your neck and cleavage. When you get to your back, start looking a little upset. Sigh prettily as you visibly fail to reach all areas. Ask nearby men for help. This is the only time when it is acceptable to go over in your knickers and bra to a strange man and ask him to massage you.

If the fat ugly women you sat next to on the beach start offering to help then pretend you can't hear them. Remember, they are just a prop.

Exiting the Sea

Your biggest moment for attracting men is your walk out of the sea. This is your catwalk runway. Get it right and it will be pure *Baywatch* as the waves lap at your ankles and you emerge, glistening from the surf, with the entire beach admiring you. Remember Ursula Andress in the first Bond film, the white bikini and the leather belt. (If you actually saw that film when it came out, you really should not be reading this book, Granny.)

Before you leave the water, we'd like you to pause when the water is at waist-height. Now turn round so your back is to the beach and you are looking out to sea. Look down. Remember you are in your bra and knickers. Make sure your bits are in place. Check if you need to move things around. Adjust all Lycra. We want you to leave the water like a young stallion. Remember, girls, you've got breasts!

Now your exit. Aim to seductively stride through the waves. Pull your stomach in, get your head up high, and think pony gymkhana as you pick up your feet, lift your knees and step over the waves. Don't try and push through the waves as you'll lose your balance and probably fall flat. If you haven't got massive breasts you could try this at a light trot. Practise before you leave for your holiday by watching the DVD of *Baywatch* to see how Pamela does it, then practice this in the bath. Get a large mirror and trot around the living room, jumping over imaginary waves and seeing if that look works for you. For added tips you can also try Bo Derek in *10*. Daniel Craig did quite a good exit in his Bond trunks, too.

Leave your flip-flops near the water's edge and head towards them during this fabulous exit. The whole thing will be ruined if you then start screaming and hopping around in agony because the sand is too hot.

And don't light a fag. Not a good look. That will kill the goddess illusion.

Beach sports

Unless you have a perfect figure, we would recommend that you steer clear of ball sports while wearing a bikini. Do something which it is easier to control your body parts in. Like shell collecting.

Reading Material

If you are reading something embarrassing like a self-help book, then change the cover. Slip something sophisticated over the top like *Sea of Lost Love* by Santa Montefiore.

Magazines and newspapers may seem like a good option but bear in mind that all the ink will come off on you – so only read while wearing dark colours. Take the magazine for the market you're looking to attract, so read *Forbes* if you want a City type, for example. Don't worry, you can have *Heat* magazine hidden inside. Don't read wedding mags or one of those awful 'How to Catch a Husband in Ten Days' books - you'll scare them off. We are, of course, perfectly acceptable beach reading. Everyone wants to date a naughty girl.

Holiday Photographs

If possible, only have photographs taken after four days in the sun so you look tanned and fabulous instead of pasty white.

Good positioning in a group shot can take at least a stone off you. Always try and get in the middle of the group as this is the most slimming and flattering position.

Link your arms round behind the waists of your two friends on either side so your bingo wings are hidden behind them. Stand slightly back so they cover part of your body. If there's someone fatter than you then get next to them.

Never hug friends around their necks as you'll end up with an unflattering shot of your armpits. Never be the person on the end of the group nearest the camera. Your arms and thighs always look fatter because you're nearest the lens. We know it's supposed to be a fun moment captured on holiday and you're not supposed to be that particular about positioning but you'll thank us when you get your pics printed and you look simply incredible.

All these tricks can help but, if at all possible, try and avoid being photographed in your bikini. If a camera is produced we suggest you strike a novelty pose, crouching playfully behind a sunbed or fellow holidaymaker in order to cover as much of your body as possible.

True friends only take head and shoulder snaps of each other while in a bikini'd state. If all else fails, then just offer to take the photographs yourself.

Drinking

We're not sure that drinking during the day really works on holiday. Remember, you are on public display in your bra and knickers. Being drunk as well is probably not a good idea. But, hey, it's your holiday and it's darn well up to you.

But we would say, from experience, that it's best to avoid wine when it's a hot summer's day. Do you honestly think you'll sip the grape seductively like a lady? More likely you'll throw it back like a truck driver, get absolutely smashed, fall asleep and wake up with a splitting headache, dry- and open-mouthed, sunburned and, if it was red, a stained red mouth and teeth that will make you look like a vampire. Trust us. Save it until the evening. Everybody else is drunk then too so you'll stand out less.

Personally, we say if you want a cheeky midday tipple then go for fruit cocktails. Take tiny sophisticated sips and think of how many vitamins you are getting.

Beauty Tips

Take full advantage of your free holiday beauty care. Nails will be whitened in the sea. Sand is a fabulous exfoliant and your teeth and eyes look brighter as you bronze. Even if you fail to get lucky on holiday, just think, you are looking more fabulous by the day, sister. You're bound to pull when you get home.

Exercise

Don't bother. A tan will take at least half a stone off you, which means that you can stuff your face all the way through your holidays and still look the same weight when you get back home. So relax and enjoy yourself.

If you do, then any exercise done on holiday proves you are an incredibly virtuous and saint-like person. You should reward yourself with vast amounts of extra calories to compensate. It's time for some maths again.

HOLIDAY EXERCISE MATHS

EXERCISE SESSION*	CALORIES ALLOWED
One brief stroll along beach holding in stomach	= 240 extra calories. E.g. three pina coladas.
Swing in hammock	= 500 extra calories. E.g. four scoops of chocolate ice cream. And some hundreds-and-thousands sprinkled on top.
Five minute half-hearted paddling session in waves	= 1,000 extra calories. E.g. two double cheeseburgers.
Two hours holding in stomach in front of very sexy group of men	= 1,100 extra calories. E.g. one bottle of wine, one Mars bar, one Scotch egg.
Snogging session on sunbed	= 1,300 extra calories. E.g. family-size pepperoni pizza.
Sex with new holiday lover	= 2,000 extra calories. E.g. Eggs Benedict and all the trimmings at The Ivy.
Jog along beach	= Oh, stop showing off. Go and eat whatever you want you smug, freaky, exercise-obsessed cow.

* Number of calories burned may not actually equal this amount, but you're worth it . . .

Holiday Romances

You must keep your standards up. Just because you've been wandering around in a bikini all day, you shouldn't start crying with relief that someone found you attractive. Don't get carried away. Stay focused. Work out if your potential suitor is worth it and that you can really hold your head up high knowing you've spent the night with him.

It's not that we don't want you to have a good time or won't forgive you for random slutty behaviour, we just want you to get it right. *Going on holiday is like being a virgin again.* Nobody on that beach knows how many men you've slept with or what your reputation's like at home. Succumb to the pig-ugly ice cream salesman by lunchtime on day one and you could ruin your chances of scoring with the local hunk on day two or three.

Here's our guide to what's acceptable:

✗ *DJs, doormen or waiters*: No. Nice as they may be, when you meet them it's probably the end of the evening and you're judgement could be flawed. If your behaviour so much as hints at sluttish you'll never be able to face that restaurant or club again. What's more, it may just be the best food or nightspot around.

✗ *Minicab drivers*: No, no, no! Just pay the fare and get out like a lady.

✗ *Cleaners, janitors, bell boys*: Please. Never with housekeeping (for further notes on when you should sleep with staff please see page 152).

? *Salesmen*: Possibly. The owner of an upmarket store or couture concession is fine and may earn you a decent discount. Sleeping with the man who sold you aloe vera on the beach that morning is not fine. It's cheap.

? *Pilots*: Debatable. Sleeping with the easyJet pilot on a short-haul flight is sluttish. The man flying your private plane, however, is more acceptable. Totally acceptable is the owner of said jet. As a basic rule, do not have sex on a commercial flight. Unless it's really long haul. And he's irresistible.

✓ *Fellow holidaymakers*: Of course this is acceptable. But ask questions first. Do they live anywhere near you? Do they know people in your office? Do you have friends in common? Basically, try and work out if you are likely to run into them again and have the tale of your wanton holiday behaviour shared with everyone at home. It's OK it if they live over a hundred miles away and you don't appear to have any mutual friends. If they own a Porsche or Ferrari do bear in mind that a hundred miles could be driven quite quickly in which case you need a good three-hundred-mile gap for safety. If however he owns a Lada then forget all these rules and go, girl, go. He'll never make the journey in that.

Finding a Holiday Lover

We suggest you take a lesson. A watersports lesson. The instructors are gorgeous and always clad in Lycra. You can buy the right to his company for an hour at a time and if you're lucky you might end up with an invitation to drinks afterwards or a chance to meet his friends.

Watersports boys are also an excellent cover story for those holiday post-mortems with the girls. If you do accidentally end up with a holiday lover who looks like something out of *The Phantom of the Opera*, then save face by getting the Lycra-clad diving/water skiing/surfing instructor to pose as your boyfriend. Simply ask him for a picture as a souvenir of his 'fabulous teaching skills'. As the camera clicks, turn and laugh happily into his face and lean in as if you are lovers. Show that photo to the girls back home and claim you slept with him. Then you can carry on seeing Quasimodo and it's your dirty little secret.

Carrying on Your Holiday Romance

Of course, the problem with being the most fabulous creature on the beach is that your holiday romance may well start begging to spend the rest of his life with you.

No matter how sexy he is, do think carefully before bringing your lover back home.

He may look unbelievably sexy dressed in rubber and doing heroic things like saving lives in the surf and battling with the sea life, but bear in mind that back home he will be doing something a bit more mundane. Ask yourself if you'd still fancy him if the only sea life he was handling was dressed crabs on the Tesco fish counter. And remember, he looks great sitting on his jet-ski all day, but get him back home and the closest he'll get to that position is perching on the loo.

Before you even think about picking up the phone and inviting him over to move in/marry you/help you bear children, we suggest you take an old photo of him in his sexy holiday gear.

Now then, cut out his head and then paste it on to these images. This is how he will look in real life back in Britain. Does he still look sexy?

If you're in any doubt about not wanting to convert your holiday romance into a permanent fixture, make sure you can easily get rid of him by never, ever giving out your exact home address. And only give your mobile number and a vague idea of where you work. Mobiles are easy to ignore. Your lover turning up on your doorstep or workplace is not. It took Sharon a month to get rid of that twenty-year-old Israeli diving instructor.

This is how he will look in real life back in Britain. Does he still look sexy?

The Naughty Girl's Mini Guide to Travelling with Her Man

If this is your first trip away with each other, remember the purpose of this trip is to con him into thinking you're a low-maintenance natural beauty and sex minx.

You're on holiday but don't relax for one second. The next few days are crucial to your relationship. He'll be watching you like a hawk to try and work out what it would be like to live with you. If you want him, you must convince the little jerk that you're perfect.

Don't panic. There are tricks of the trade. We'll tell you how.

Luggage

You're a girl, so you can take lots of luggage. But don't freak him out. You're not Elizabeth Taylor. It shouldn't be necessary to hire a separate plane for your luggage. Do this and he'll start panicking that if you ever move in together you'll be shoving aside his boy stuff and loading the place up with knickers. So go easy. You can always buy new stuff when you get there.

Now, we know the temptation on the first night is to drag out your best outfit. You'll have just got off the plane, grey and tired, and the place will be filled with bronzed goddesses who have spent days on sunbeds and are now looking fabulously relaxed and healthy. You'll want to distract him with your best showstopping frock and dress up as shiny as a little Christmas cracker. Don't. Go for something dark and slimming and simple – your favourite and reliable Little Black Dress perhaps – and do a careful make-up job to try and drag his attention to your face and away from your sunless body. Save that hot outfit for ammunition later on. Remember, he'll be tired from the flight too. All he really wants is a cold beer and a hot cuddle.

Packing

Make sure that you pack some emergency first aid stuff like plasters, aftersun and diarrhoea tablets. Men always end up cutting themselves, burning and getting a dodgy tummy on holiday and you can simply swoop into your suitcase and emerge as his own personal Florence Nightingale.

Take some nice oils, and perhaps some bedroom equipment too. You're on holiday. You can stay in bed all day if you want. Let him know that you're a wanton sex goddess. Bear in mind that you might get searched at Customs though, so don't go over the top. You want to come across as a sex kitten, not a sales rep from Ann Summers.

It's good to have some nice baby wipes. Keep them in the loo. We're sure we don't need to spell this out, ladies, but it's hot out there and baby-bottom fresh is what we're aiming for.

Pack a scented candle too. And some matches. We'll explain why in a tick.

Pre-trip Beauty Preparation

You are about to take your man into an environment where women will be walking about in bikinis and several may well be thinner than you. You must prepare for battle.

Let's start with waxing. As we've said before, it needs to be hardcore. Check in the magnifying mirror for any resistant rogues.

Do NOT have a spray tan before you go on holiday. It won't make you look fabulous and bronzed, it'll make you look odd. What looks great in the UK will just be orange in the bright harsh light of a foreign sun. And there are bound to be patches that have been missed. No man wants to spend his time lying on the beach next to something resembling a hyena. If you really, really want a bit of colour, then we say ignore the health warnings just this once and go for a sunbed.

Sulking

Face facts. Your man is bound to ogle other women on the beach. Deal with it. Do not panic. Do not be neurotic. Do not accuse him of flirting. Men hate confrontation. If you start getting defensive he'll deny it and instead of just staring at other women's breasts, thinking they are better than yours, he will stare at other women thinking that they have better breasts *and* are much less of a nag.

Tell yourself that you're in a place filled with half-naked women. Of course he's going to want a bit of a peek. Don't worry about it. Just get yourself some nice dark shades so you can secretly stare at all the boys.

If any girl is presenting a massive threat simply befriend her during your holiday. Go over to her for a casual chat at some point on your own. When you come back to your man, sigh heavily and say, 'Oh God. That's so tragic. She's so beautiful, too.' When he asks what you're talking about tell him that she's come out on holiday to get over the heartache of discovering that her ex has given her herpes.

Apartment Etiquette

You've got to be tidy. He's watching what you do to the pristine hotel room and converting it into what you might do to any home you live in together. So don't go leaving soggy sandy swimsuits on the floor or filling the place with empty bottles.

Of course, it is perfectly acceptable to fling any clothing to the floor during a moment of abandoned passion. In fact, we absolutely demand it. For goodness' sake don't start interrupting everything by folding your pants and putting his socks in pairs. Just be conscious that leaving the room full of girlie things like knickers, tights and hair removal cream will frighten him.

If you really can't be bothered, then bribe housekeeping to come in and do some overtime.

Bathroom Etiquette

Do not leave all your make-up around the bathroom. Remember you're a natural beauty, so hide all the foundations, concealers, tweezers, etc. away in your suitcase. Just leave a little powder-brush out on the dressing table and perhaps some lip gloss and let the idiot think that's all you use.

Do not, under any circumstances, leave out any girlie

pharmaceuticals. Thrush cream is not a good

look. Maintain your mystique.

It is also essential, ladies, that we work to keep the en suite sweet.

Now, remember, he's a man. He won't even think twice about bottom etiquette. He may poo with abandon but this is not your cue to do the same.

You're a lady. OK, when you gotta go, you gotta go, but if at all possible don't go in the en suite. If you're in a hotel, claim you're just off to check something with housekeeping, then head up the corridor, find another loo and go in there and the rest is up to you.

If that's not an option, and you have to go in your hotel bathroom, then flush as soon as possible. Mid-action if possible. Then grab the matches we said you should pack and light one of those. If you've got the trots and have spent the day glued to the loo then light a candle to provide a permanent flame to try and disguise things. Do not spray your scent in the air. This actually makes things worse. Don't be ashamed. It could be him tomorrow.

Getting Drunk

Of course we know you're on holiday, of course we understand you want to sample the occasional cocktail, but if he has to carry you back to the room because you're throwing up on rum punches then it's not good. It will only lead to arguments.

We'd never nag you to go teetotal but suggest you steer towards tipsy at most. If you go partying, match your input with a glass of water and don't, under any circumstances, mix your drinks. Go out in super high heels and stand up at all times. When you can no longer balance on your skyscrapers it's time to go home.

Now if you don't manage this, go too far and wake up one morning realising you were a really horrible embarrassingly drunk girlfriend the night before, then it's time to take action. Don't worry if you just ogled men or flirted. That is perfectly acceptable and, as long as you have woken up with your man and no one else, you are OK and you are forgiven.

If you made an unexpected body emission, engaged in public nudity or snogged or groped the waiter then we're really sorry but, no matter how rough you feel, you're going to have to take immediate remedial action. Unless you want to carry a big shame stick for the rest of your trip then it's a 999 situation. As soon as you physically can, get out of bed, go to the bathroom, clean your teeth, brush your tongue, wipe the mascara out of your eyes. It is soooo unchic to apologise looking like a panda. Give yourself a good talking to in the mirror.

Saunter back into that bedroom smelling daisy fresh and looking like a lady. **Then get down on your knees and stop being a lady. Soften the blow!** Preferably before he wakes up and remembers last night's fiasco.

Now, we know we told you not to do it, but don't beat yourself up too much about a bad drinking experience. Tell him you've mixed alcohol with medication. Suggest you were jet-lagged. Mention something hormonal. Tell him you think your drink may have been spiked. If you've taken action and asked for forgiveness then he should give in. Don't let him sulk or brood about it for more than two days.

Of course, if the tables are turned and he humiliated you in public then you should make him pay, in a manner you enjoy, every day for the rest of the trip before you even start to think about forgiving him. New shoes are always nice, too.

NB: By humiliated, we mean he flirted slightly with someone. If he did something totally unacceptable like kissing them, we suggest you pack up the hotel room and check out of the relationship. Take his passport, airline tickets, cash and all of his clothes as a souvenir.

What You Want Out of Your Holiday

As a singleton, you're after a fabulous tan and hopefully another name to add to your list of men that didn't count. If you're travelling as a couple, use all our tips for conning him that you're a goddess but also use them to work out if you want to be with him for longer.

What you're after, ideally, is a blissful two weeks with nothing above a light bicker and a low count on the scale of unavoidable body functions. **If he's managed this then you may well be on to a winner, girls.**

In fact, we say if he did any of the following keep hold of him and forgive whatever state he left the en suite in:

CHECKLIST
- ❏ *Told you that you looked fantastic in your bikini.*
- ❏ *Offered to give you a massage.*
- ❏ *Pointed out another girl on the beach who had worse cellulite than you.*

❏ *Chuckled indulgently at you when you got drunk.*

❏ *Rubbed all your suncream in for you.*

❏ *Went off to get you lots of fattening ice creams, pastas and cocktails. Without once pointing out the calorie content.*

❏ *Only looked at the thin woman with the fabulous breasts when he thought you were asleep.*

PART SEVEN:

The Naughty Girl in the Spotlight

PRAYER

Grant me the serenity to accept celebrities are a shallow,
insecure and self-obsessed breed

Courage not to despair if some of them sit there
Googling themselves all day

And the wisdom to realise that underneath all that
they're actually not so bad, and A-list often equals
a car when it comes to pressies.

The Naughty Girl's Guide to Celebrities

Celebrities are so pampered and employ so many hangers-on, they often think they are the second coming. Remember, they are not. They are just someone off the telly.

However, they are very useful. Here's how to work for them, play with them, and use and abuse them.

For the purpose of this chapter we define 'celebrity' as anyone who is invited to do shoots in *OK!* magazine, has appeared on Parky or who makes the national newspapers every time they sleep with somebody new. Someone who has uploaded a video on YouTube, appeared on *Jerry Springer* or who got into the newspapers because they slept with Dean Gaffney does not count.

The Fan's Guide to Meeting a Celebrity

Everyone thinks they have to be really cool when meeting celebrities. They should nod, be dignified and pretend not to really know who they are. This is nonsense. Secretly, celebrities want you to bring it on. Stars just LOVE being fawned over. There's no need to go for an embarrassing all-out gush, but a bit of enthusiasm and prior research is always greatly appreciated.

The following is perfectly acceptable behaviour. Stand outside Chinawhites, Nobus, The Ivy, or at award ceremonies and try these tips. If applied correctly, the celebrity should reward you with a small memento of themselves – an autograph, a photograph or an offer of casual sex.

CHECKLIST

❑ *Tell them they look better in the flesh. Meeting your chosen celebrity for the first time is a bit like seeing a brochure of a great hotel. When you look at the real thing, as opposed to the airbrushed image, it's never quite as clean, as big, as sparkling or as fabulous. Remember this when you meet your celebrity. Do not allow your face to fall as you realise that, in the cold, brutal make-up free light of day, they look dog rough. Steel yourself before meeting your celeb.* **You might well be disappointed when you meet them. But don't tut, sigh or cry.**

❑ *For women, if they have a particular female celebrity rival on the telly, it's always a good move to sidle over to them and say, 'I saw (insert name of arch rival) last week. She's grown a moustache and she definitely needs her roots doing.' If the female celeb asks you to go on, then add that the person also looked really tired and had put on weight. And add that she was a bit of a cow, quite frankly.*

❑ *For men, say you noticed a bald patch on their rival's head. And that he was developing man boobs. And you're pretty sure he had lifts in his shoes.*

❑ *Try and rack your brains for something that they've done and tell them that watching/cooking/listening to it changed your life. Include details like a beaten addiction,*

a mended marriage or perhaps a dying pet that rallied when the celeb appeared on telly. Celebs love hearing things like this. It'll give them something to boast about when they're next on Parky.

❑ Bringing gifts is always a good move if you want to stand out amongst the crowd of adoring fans. Every celeb gets lots of freebies but nobody's ever going to object to a couple more. Gifts with steering wheels and sunroofs are especially lovely and a really nice touch. If you're skint then offer fresh flowers or perhaps a head massage. It's the thought that counts. If you're pushed for time just give a compliment. Tell them they've lost weight and look fabulous. Even the size zero skinny ones always like to hear they've lost even more.

❑ If it's George Michael don't bother doing any of this, just grow a handlebar moustache and hang out in Hampstead Heath.* He'll introduce himself soon.
  * This rule applies to boys only.

❑ Be equipped. If you want them to sign something, put a bit of effort into it. All celebrities will happily sign any book of theirs that you happen to be carrying. If you simply want the autograph to flog on eBay then obviously you'll have to avoid them personalising it and ruining its value. Be inventive. Don't say, 'No, don't write my name, I'll never be able to sell it.' This annoys celebrities. Say it's for a charity auction. They will then happily sign as this makes them feel they are 'giving something back'.

❑ If you have spotted the celeb in the loos then it is unacceptable to approach them while they are in a state of undress. Even if they are behind a closed door and you can't see them. Let them finish, flush, zip, wash and dry

their hands and only approach as they finish checking
their reflection in the mirror. *

* This rule does not apply to George Michael if you are a
boy or in the LAPD.

❑ *Do ask the celebrity if you can take a photograph. It's*
really obvious when people hold up a mobile phone,
pretend to be typing a message and start framing up the
celeb in the camera. The phone goes 'click' for a start.
And a big flashing light comes on, which is a giveaway.
Of course you should ask in a way that doesn't let them
say no. The best approach is to have the camera or phone
pointing and ready, and say, 'Oh, I must get a picture for
my dying relative/pet/friend, she's such a fan and thinks
you're fabulous,' and click away as you speak. If the
celeb stops the shot after an intro like that, then they're
pigs and don't deserve your praise. Get your own back by
telling them they've put on weight. Or that you're terribly
sorry, you mistook them for Vanessa Feltz.

The Celebrities' Guide to Meeting Fans

Celebs come and go. Think Steve Brookstein. You need to work to keep your adoring public adoring you and make sure you earn their lasting love when you meet them.

In your first year of fame we accept that you're probably not going to behave. If you're really ugly then you're bound to find it difficult to resist when people suddenly want to sleep with you. So for twelve months after first finding fame we say do what you like. Sleep with your groupies, sleep with faded soap stars, sleep with a mother/daughter combo if you like. Develop addictions and be described by the tabloids as 'troubled'. After that it's time to give up. Remember, you're not getting kudos any more. You're just getting herpes.

Here's the checklist for good grown-up celebrity behaviour:

CHECKLIST

☐ *Do not make any body emissions in front of your fans. David Hasselhoff once loosened quite a lot of phlegm in front of Sharon without warning and it absolutely ruined a twenty-year infatuation. Remember, when you're meeting your public you are selling a dream.*

☐ *Garlic's out. And deodorant and mouthwash are in. It's better your fans remember you by your face, not your smell.*

☐ *Do sign autographs. Nobody's ever so important or busy that they cannot write their name. If you've got a really long name just scribble your initials, you lazy git. If you really can't be bothered just wrap your writing hand up in bandages and wave it with a winsome smile at your disappointed fans. They'll forgive you.*

☐ *Do take an interest. If it's a premiere and people have been standing outside for hours in the freezing cold then don't walk straight past them into your comfy, warm cinema seat. Offer to rub their hands, loan your scarf, give them hot water bottles. On the red carpet it's always good PR to be seen shedding a good few layers of clothing in this way. It's actually worth coming wrapped up like a little polar bear as you arrive so that you can* spontaneously hand out items to the adoring crowds. Give them all a little memento of you.

❑ Do give generously to beggars. Come on, you miserable tight-fists. You earn a squillion pounds a year and get applauded for walking into a room. The least you can do is hand over a fiver.

❑ Diva behaviour is out. Unless it's funny or interesting. Demands for repainted walls and refusals to be looked in the eye and temper tantrums are so passé. If you're going to be a diva then at least make it entertaining. Ask for a school of porpoises to chant you to sleep at night or for kittens to be dyed to match your pubic hair or for goldfish in your Evian water. One A-lister absolutely refused to make his live appearance on This Morning until everyone had agreed to play hide and seek with him. He was found – thirty seconds before he was due on air – fully dressed and hiding in the shower.

❑ It is unacceptable to hit staff. Even if you're Naomi Campbell and really beautiful.

❑ DON'T sleep with Rebecca Loos. You'll look cheap.*
  * This applies to girls and boys.

Working for Celebrities

Working for celebrities is not as fabulous as it may seem. OK, there is a good chance you'll end up with a Christmas gift beginning with the letter c – Cartier, cars, caviar or cocaine. But you should also bear in mind that you'll be on twenty-four-hour call to the demanding little idiot and they're usually too thick to understand time differences. We know of one particularly challenged rock star who rang from the

Chateau Marmont in LA to his PA in her English bed to complain that the staff had put pickle on his hamburger. It was 2 a.m.

This sort of behaviour is, we're afraid, normal. You're much better off just sleeping with one.

Dating Celebrities

If you insist on netting a celebrity, all you have to do is ask nicely. Hang about

outside Chinawhites and you could be horizontal with an ex-*EastEnder* by first light.

If you really want to *date* a celebrity, then it's different. Use a subtle approach. Undress that stud muffin with your eyes, not your hands, and remember to point out that you're over the age of consent, too. It'll set you apart from the rest of his fans.

If, on the other hand, you are going to have a celebrity bang for the sake of the celebrity bang, we're hoping you wouldn't consider anyone that hadn't made it on to Parky's guest list. As for bagging Hollywood A-list celebrities, it doesn't necessarily mean you're easy, it just means you've got really good taste.

There are lots of advantages to dating a celebrity. You get to see all the movies before anyone else, you get given free drinks and people from TV reality shows air kiss you and want to be your friend. Glossy magazines call to ask to do gushing features on you. The resulting photographs will make you look much thinner, sweat-free and smooth-skinned than you ever were in real life.

But remember, one false move and it's all over. You'll be back to paying for your own drinks, all the Z-listers will blank you and the only phone calls you'll get will be from the tabloids asking if there's any chance you'll pose in your knickers and bra and sell the 'story of your heartache'.

Just in case it ever happens, here's the code of conduct for dating a celebrity.

AIRBRUSHING

Understand and appreciate that airbrushing goes on. Before you see your celebrity lover naked for the first time, we suggest you get ready by sitting in front of a mirror and practising not looking disappointed. It is incredibly bad form to stare at said lover in the nude and say in a crestfallen voice, 'Oh, you didn't look like that in the movie/pop video/underwear ad.'

Help them. Prepare the room and lower the lights – add flattering candles – and force yourself to smile appreciatively as they get undressed. Understand that if they are undressing after an event at which they have been photographed, it is entirely likely that they will be clad in massive layers of slimming Lycra pants, have lifts in their shoes and perhaps some padding. Do not recoil as they disrobe. Or wince. You will just upset them.

MEMORABILIA

Before your new celebrity lover comes round to your house, we suggest you hide any DVDs/posters/books of theirs that you own.

If you've got a shrine to them in your bedroom, dismantle it and hide it. This sort of thing will scare them. You should

especially make sure you have removed any posters which contain evidence of wear and tear where you've been snogging them. If you've got their name tattooed on your skin, we suggest you camouflage it.

You should also have a quick check through any reading material which is out on display in your home. If it consists of *OK!*, *Hello!*, *Heat* and every tabloid newspaper, you may look like a bit of a celebrity wannabe. Go out and buy a few copies of *Horse and Hound*, *Interiors* and *Top Gear*. At least it will show you've got interests beyond leading a shallow celebrity lifestyle.

THE RED CARPET

Non-celebrity dates should remember that the red carpet is not your carpet. We know this is harsh but when you turn up at a showbiz do with your celebrity boyfriend the best thing you can do is imagine that the carpet is beige and you are wearing muddy shoes. Don't step on it. You will only get it dirty.

Nothing looks worse than the unknown partner desperately clinging on to the arm of the celebrity as the star tries to manoeuvre their way down the red carpet.

The fans have come to see your date, paw your date and try and even get off with your date. They will only hate you if you stand smugly by his side looking patronisingly at them. They will hate you even more if you start running up the carpet and hitting the adoring fans and yelling, 'He's mine!'

Remember you are going home with the celebrity, possibly to a nice warm bed tonight. Those poor fans have been queuing for hours in the freezing cold merely to share his airspace.

Just be generous and let them live their moment.

Likewise, you should appreciate that the press photographers and camera crews are all trying to get a clear shot of your man without you in tow. This is so they can trash his outfit/hairstyle later on. You will annoy everyone if you persist on taking his arm and getting into shot. If you are specifically invited over by the camera crews, ask yourself why they want to photograph you. Do a quick check to see if anything's popped out. Then go over, do one smile for the cameras before graciously exiting, saying they should photograph your partner as it is 'his night'.

Ideally, you shouldn't actually be seen at all. The best thing for you to do is stand at the top of the carpet and let your date go off and be admired by his adoring fans. Then sidle round the back and catch up with him inside. He will reward you with a nice big hug and kiss for being such an understanding and non-fame-seeking partner. Of course, you should use the hug as a cover to quickly search his pockets to remove any telephone numbers that may have been slipped in by any adoring fans.

If you are a non-celebrity, the only time you are allowed up the red carpet alongside your lover is if you have just announced your engagement or if you are pregnant (by him). Friendship rings and slightly late periods do not count.

PAPARAZZI

Early on in the dating procedure you should aim to stay out of paparazzi photographs. No matter how gorgeous your man is, never ever jump proudly into shot when a pap takes his photograph. Beaming broadly, or even worse, snogging him when caught by the cameras for the first time, just makes you look desperate. Or really, really pleased with yourself for pulling above your usual rank. It is not acceptable to squeeze into shot – even if you are wearing a particularly splendid new dress.

Of course, we're not saying you should run away in horror, shrieking, 'Paps! Paps!' He might feel you're ashamed to be seen with him if you do this. Instead just continue to walk by his side, perhaps lightly holding on to his arm, with a calm expression on your face. Don't talk to the paparazzi. Do not start giving out business cards. We suggest you concentrate on trying to look sober, dignified and unaffected.

It's time for maths again.

CELEBRITY DATING MATHS

For the first month of dating, it is only really acceptable to have fifteen per cent of your body in any press photograph of your famous lover.

This equals one shoulder, a hand and perhaps an ear.

If any more of your body appears in the pic, then you have clearly been clinging to him like a desperate wannabe and you really need to get a grip.

Bearing this in mind, before leaving the house, you should examine all these extraneous body parts and see if they are fit to appear in the mags. Have a fabulous manicure, some nice cuffs and chose some lovely earrings. You may wish to spend extra time in the weights section of the local gym building up your biceps. It would be a disaster if all that appeared in print was a big close-up of your bingo wings.

PHOTOGRAPHS

As a rule, we'd say you shouldn't really take any photographs of your celebrity date for at least a month. We know this sounds hard but grabbing your mobile and snapping him as he lies next to you will make him think you're preparing to flog the story of your 'great romance' or that he's landed himself in the middle of an *OK!* photo shoot.

Of course, if things don't look like they're going to last and he's being a bit of a swine to you, then ignore this rule.

We don't approve of kiss and tells, but if you really must and he's being a pig and deserves it, then bear in mind that you will need a souvenir photo of him at some stage. We suggest you wait until he goes to sleep and snap him then, looking relaxed and, well, unimpressive. This of course should fetch a higher price later on. We do admit that this sort of behaviour is pretty extreme and only to be resorted to if he has behaved like a complete rotter, bounder, and all-round love rat.

Should you, on the other hand, wish to win the trust of your celebrity trophy, make a huge fuss about deleting any naked telephone photographs or embarrassing text messages prior to a big night out at a press-packed party. Make a show of deleting everything in front of him to prove your sincerity, saying, 'Gosh, better get rid of that, can you IMAGINE what would happen if I dropped my phone tonight? That would be soooo awful.'

This should only be done once you have shown absolutely everything to the girls, and forwarded the really saucy ones for safe-keeping and unimagined eventualities.

INVITATIONS

If you go round to their house and see a host of invitations addressed to them 'plus one', don't presume you are that plus one and excitedly grab it and start talking about what you're going to wear. Definitely do not turn up on the day of the event wearing a ballgown and an expectant smile on your face. Wait to be asked. He may be planning to take his mother, his agent, his sister, or, if you're very unlucky, his wife.

CLOTHES

Never, ever aim
to upstage
your
celebrity lover
at a photocall.
Turning up with no
clothes on may have
worked for Liz Hurley all those
years ago but there's no guarantee it'll
get you an Estée Lauder contract too. Liz
was lucky.

Try that sort of stunt at his premiere and the
only contract you're likely to end up with is a
restraining order asking you to leave him alone.

Please also remember that the camera flash
can make fabrics like chiffon totally
transparent, which means that instead of
everyone seeing your lovely girlie dress,
they see your massive hold-it-all-in
knickers and big sturdy bra. It's
worth a test run at home using a
friend with a flash camera and a
big torch to check that
nothing undesired will be
on show during your
moment of glory.

THE NEWSPAPERS

Don't make a big song and
dance about the newspapers

ringing you up or asking you questions in the street. There's really no need to do a Heather Mills and start videoing them all and complaining. **Be honest, you love it really.** The Press Complaints Commission has better things to do.

Be nice to the reporters who turn up, ask their names and tell them you're really sorry but they'll have to go via your partner and/or his agent on this one. This allows you to warn your celebrity boyfriend exactly which papers are currently being briefed to come up with a story about you. It also gives you a wide range of press contacts should your celebrity lover ever humiliate you by sleeping with the nanny and you wish to sell your story.

On the subject of newspapers, if you receive a phone call or text message out of the blue from some cast-off, disgruntled, long-forgotten former lover to discuss your 'night of passion', whether it rings a bell or not, tell them you have no idea what they're referring to and hang up immediately. Nine times out of ten they'll be sitting in the office of some pesky national newspaper journalist who will be recording every word you say. Any of your dewy-eyed reminiscences would not make good reading for your lover as he works his way through your carefully prepared bacon and eggs on Sunday morning.

And, incidentally, should they be ringing with details of a particularly regrettable episode from your carefree youth, just think hard and try and remember if it was videoed! If not, deny everything.

PET NAMES
Don't use pet names in public. In our opinion, it all started going downhill for Beckham after 'Goldenballs'.

SELLING OUT ON YOUR CELEBRITY

Flogging your story will make you look most undignified, girls, and we are soooo against it. Straddling two pages of a downmarket tabloid in your knickers will not launch you on the road to stardom. It'll simply make you look like a complete tart. If you're harbouring doubts, we suggest you Google Alicia Douvall and Rebecca Loos and see what it did for them.

So, as a rule it's NO to selling out. OK, if he cheated on you horribly and did something completely and indescribably appalling, we can understand you obviously want to get your own back. In very exceptional cases, having considered every other option open to you and having decided to resort to the unspeakable, you will need to work out how much you are going to charge.

The starting point is at least a few grand, then add a further five thousand if you can answer 'yes' to any of the following questions about the soon-to-be-betrayed.

CHECKLIST

- ☐ *Is he still in Madame Tussauds? On display. Not in the back being melted.*
- ☐ *Did he travel in style? By that we mean did he automatically turn left on entering an aeroplane? (This question does not apply to private jets.) On the subject of which, did he own his Jetstream or Lear? NetJets is OK. easyJet not so good. Bus or ferry? Look, we thought we told you to leave those ex-*EastEnders *alone.*
- ☐ *Are there streets named after him?*
- ☐ *Do tourist buses stop outside his house?*
- ☐ *Was his mantelpiece weighed down with glamorous invitations? A Bafta? An Ivor Novello? An Oscar? Some*

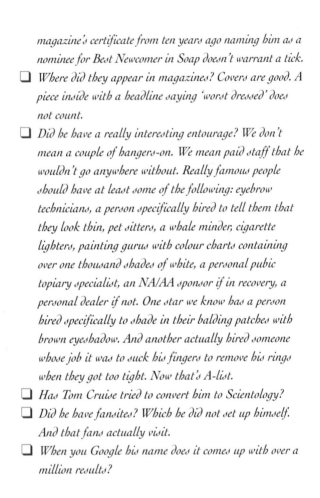

magazine's certificate from ten years ago naming him as a
nominee for Best Newcomer in Soap doesn't warrant a tick.

❑ *Where did they appear in magazines? Covers are good. A
piece inside with a headline saying 'worst dressed' does
not count.*

❑ *Did he have a really interesting entourage? We don't
mean a couple of hangers-on. We mean paid staff that he
wouldn't go anywhere without. Really famous people
should have at least some of the following: eyebrow
technicians, a person specifically hired to tell them that
they look thin, pet sitters, a whale minder, cigarette
lighters, painting gurus with colour charts containing
over one thousand shades of white, a personal pubic
topiary specialist, an NA/AA sponsor if in recovery, a
personal dealer if not. One star we know has a person
hired specifically to shade in their balding patches with
brown eyeshadow. And another actually hired someone
whose job it was to suck his fingers to remove his rings
when they got too tight. Now that's A-list.*

❑ *Has Tom Cruise tried to convert him to Scientology?*

❑ *Did he have fansites? Which he did not set up himself.
And that fans actually visit.*

❑ *When you Google his name does it comes up with over a
million results?*

If you're really savage, we suggest you ring up the newspapers and
arrange to do one of those stories where 'a friend' spills the beans
on your behalf, going on about how patient, long-suffering, pretty,
bright, amusing, indispensable, entertaining, etc. you were
throughout, and what a complete jerk he was to you and how he
needs his head examined for dumping you.

If you continue ignoring our advice and are determined to sink to the lowest depths possible, and just happen to have some incriminating video footage somewhere which you are prepared to use á la Paris Hilton, just stick a zero on the end.

Don't pose for photographs in the newspaper. Instead ask to have one of those paparazzi-type shots of you being 'caught unaware as you leave the house'. And please try and make it look realistic – don't emerge mid-morning wearing ballgown couture complete with full make-up.

Of course, everyone will know it was you that flogged the story but you'll just have to go on denying it and say you haven't got the faintest idea how it all got into the press. Then pocket the cash.

You can ring the *Sun* now on 020 7782 4000.

PART EIGHT:

The Naughty Girl on a Diet

PRAYER

Grant us the serenity to understand that as we
grow up, our bums grow out

Courage to accept when the varicose veins have kicked in

And the wisdom to know that life is about
counting our friends – not our calories.

The Naughty Girl's Mini Guide to Big Bottoms

Are You Too Fat?

You've turned to the chapter marked diet. Are you perhaps under the impression that your bum is too big? Now, before we get on to anything horrendous like eating plans or gym regimes, we'd like you to just stop for one moment and think. How fat are you really? Are you, for example, in the *Guinness Book of Records* under the 'Fat' section? Has a documentary crew turned up on your doorstep in the past six months saying they'd like to film you, and mentioned that the film's title contains the words 'World's Biggest'?

Did you meet your last partner via a website headed 'Feeders'? Or did you lose your last partner in a crevice? NB: Have you tried unrolling every limb? You might find him.

Do you tend to eat more than one livestock creature in an average 'snack'? If any of these do apply to you then we suggest you cut down the food intake a touch, if you can. Try not to eat more than you can lift. Oh, and do avoid patterns. They'll make your bottom look even bigger.

If none of the above apply then cheer up. You're not really that fat.

We know you're still in doubt so we suggest you apply a simple test. Buy yourself some black and white striped pants. Go out and find a zebra crossing and lie down next to it. Compare yourself to the road. If the stripes on your bottom are the same size as the stripes next to you then this is not good. If people start walking on you instead of the crossing then it's also a sign that you may be a little on the plump side.*

If not, then you're just normal. So stop worrying and read on. If you'd like to be thinner then simply do five firm butt clenches at the end of every chapter. Read us enough and we'll leave you with buns of steel.

Meanwhile, here are a few tips for the wobbly bits.

Clothes

There's nothing wrong with having a bit of junk in your trunk. Curves are good.

There's no use spending your life trying to look like a supermodel and thinking that will make your life perfect. As we've pointed out before, we know of at least one supermodel who's been prescribed all manner of creams for her down-below bits – so you see, even if you are thin and pretty on the outside, you can still have issues. Now, back to the point. Assuming you don't regularly grace the cover of *Vogue* – and if you do then please stop reading us and being so smug – here are some dressing tips for mere mortals.

Strip off. Look in the mirror and look hard. There will be one point of you that's good. We're not going to accept that you can't find anything at all. We're sure you don't go around with a

* By the way, do not attempt this during rush hour.

Balenciaga bag over your head the whole time. Everybody has at least one point about their body which is fabulous.

Think hard. It doesn't matter if all you can think of are your feet. A lot of men out there have foot fetishes so just get yourself a good pedicure, buy some open-toed mules and go out there and display.

If your tootsies are all gnarled and hobbit-like then work upwards. How are the breasts? Have you a pert nose? Shiny hair? A good manicurist? Have you been particularly meticulous about your bikini-line waxing? Do you have above average earlobes?

Now if you can – and we accept this may be difficult if your strong point is your hidden hairline – show this bit off at all times. Meanwhile, here's a quick checklist to dressing:

CHECKLIST

✓ *When trying on a new outfit do up all zips then check to see if you can pick something up off the floor. If you pass out, it's too tight.*

✓ *Do check out your bottom in the mirror. How tightly is the material straining at the seams? Do you look like a sofa? Go one size up – it's OK. You can cut the label out.*

✓ *When shopping for problem clothes which never fit, like jeans, we recommend you take one item into the changing rooms which is at least three sizes too big for you. Slip it on, watch the way it hangs off you and cheer as you remind yourself that at least you're not that fat. This will give you strength and confidence later on and make you less likely to cry when you cannot get anything to pull up further than your knees.*

✓ *Always buy from America if possible. Their dress sizes are two sizes larger than ours, giving you an instant feeling of skinniness.*

✓ *Spray tans give an immediate illusion of weight loss, as do high heels.*

✓ *Vertical stripes do NOT give the same illusion no matter what the style books say. They just make you look like a big fat zebra. Go for solid black instead.*

✓ *Thongs should never be worn on anyone over a size zero or they will get lost in the lard. This rule applies to everybody. Even if they've just been voted Rear of the Year. Go for French knickers instead.*

✓ *Don't get too hung up on dieting. If we're being honest you might like to know we're writing this chapter eating a plate of profiteroles, having devoured a Chinese takeaway, and we're washing it down with a bottle of wine.*

✓ *We are doing bum clenches though.*

✓ *And remember, you're not really fat, so don't get depressed. Take a photo of yourself today. In ten years' time you will look back at yourself and think you weren't that old, you weren't that fat and wonder why on earth you worried so much. You look great. If you don't believe us then go dig out a photo taken of yourself ten years ago that you hated and see how fabulous you looked. Now whack on some make-up, hoist up your bra and get out there and enjoy yourself. Remember, you'll never look this young again.*

Don't forget there are minus points to being thin, too. Thin girls have nothing up top and get cold all the time. They have to spend a fortune on boob jobs and cashmere.

Are You Too Skinny?

Of course it can all go the other way too and there are lots of us girls who are just too skinny.

Again, there are plus points to every situation. If you are skinny you may have to invest in cashmere but save cash by buying your T-shirts at Mothercare. Plus, if you haven't got boobs, you can run around without bits bouncing about in your face. And plane economy seats will actually seem quite roomy.

There is one minus point about being thin as TPT can testify. People think it's perfectly fine to come up to you and say, 'You are far too skinny at the moment.' It's a double standard. If people do this, remember you are perfectly within your rights to turn round and tell them they're too fat/old. Or just deck them. If they're being that rude to you then the one thing you don't have to bite is your tongue.

Exercise Bores

If there's one thing we hate it's an exercise bore. You know the type that does iron man triathlons 'for fun'. Go to the gym by all means – but please just obey a few simple rules.

✓ Do not stay naked in communal changing rooms for more than five minutes. Maximum. Those cellulite-free women who sit there smugly rubbing in body butter, making phone calls and generally showing off their neat little firm bodies just make us want to vomit. If you're sitting somewhere in public naked and reading our book then please put on some knickers and kindly stop swanking.

Never wear hotpants either. Stick to loose-fitting stuff.

✓ Never buy light-coloured trousers to wear for training sessions. Even if they are in the sale. Dark sweat stains are not a good look and can be misleading. Stick to black.

✓ Never wear hotpants either. Even if you look like a racehorse in them when you're trying them on in the changing rooms, anything more than a light trot will have your bottom wobbling about all over the place like a little hippo. Stick to loose-fitting stuff. Exercise is the only time we'll let you off looking your usual stylish self. Scrape your hair up, wipe off the make-up, and sweat. Remember it is absolutely acceptable to look like s*** when you're working out.

✓ Do not bang on about your gym routine to non gym-goers. The girls in the office are not in the least bit interested in how heavy the weights are or how many steps you can do on the stepper machine. Save this stuff for your gym instructor. The only thing that is permissible is to go on about how stiff you feel the day after exercise in order that everyone else can feel smug and superior having stayed in eating chocolate on the sofa.

✓ Do hire the fittest and best-looking gym instructor you can find. If you're going to go through agony you may as well have something nice in tight Lycra to look at, and it may make you try harder.

✓ Don't try and bed the personal trainer, though. This is such a cliché and besides, if things go wrong, you won't train any more and you'll end up looking like a blob. You're much better off booking a relaxing massage after your training session and bagging the masseur instead.

How to Exercise if You Can't be Arsed

Of course, the one downside to going to the gym is that you do actually have to do some exercise. **If you want all the admiration that goes with starting a gym routine, but none of the actual effort, then we recommend you fake it.**

This can be done during office hours, involves no more than five minutes of physical exertion and will earn you hours of praise.

Take some running gear to work and change into it at around about 11 a.m., walking through the office so everyone notices you and you can announce your intention to exercise. If they're not paying any attention, maybe do a few light stretches over the photocopier until somebody finally notices.

Just before 1 p.m. start to make your way out of the building. Any later and people may have actually left the office to start getting their lunch and may miss your big exit. It is also the time when the maximum number of smokers will be gathered on the steps outside, all debating where they should go for lunch. This will ensure the largest possible audience for your 'exercise session'.

Skip past the smokers and down any stairs at a light trot. Wave at people you know, but signal that you can't stop to talk as you're off for a run. Sprint down the street as fast as you can and take the first available corner. **Then take the first available bus or tube.**

Aim to travel at least three tube stops or four bus stops away from your office, then disembark and go for a nice leisurely lunch. Eat something that will not drip – choose penne over spaghetti, for example – as turning up with half your lunch down your top will be a dead giveaway. Also avoid garlic or anything that might linger on your breath and expose your little lunchtime secret.

We'd also say avoid alcohol if you can. Coming back with signs of wine will ruin the whole thing. If you really must then choose vodka which will not show on the breath.

Now it's time to come back to the office. Return by public transport and then pause round the corner and prepare. Check there are no crumbs on your top, drip a little water on your hair and rub your hands over your eyes to smudge your mascara. If there was any olive oil available over lunch then you could apply this to your hairline to complete that authentic runner's 'glow'.

Sprint back up the final stretch, up through the smokers and back to your office. For added effect take the stairs if you feel able to but this may be asking the impossible. Taking the lift and collapsing 'exhausted' against the walls after your massive run is also perfectly acceptable.

Safely back in the office, make a huge show of 'stretching' as you receive compliments from your colleagues. Lie on the floor to make it really noticeable. Remember to be out of breath whenever anybody talks to you for at least five minutes– there's no point sitting there in a pool of sweat and cheerily saying 'Hi'. You want to look sufficiently knackered that your colleagues rally round and start fetching you water and cups of tea, and even rubbing your tired legs.

You can then spend the rest of the day being congratulated and also not have to bother to do anything that involves any physical exertion – like tidying shelves, fetching files or going on coffee/fag runs. This is because you can claim you're 'just so knackered I can barely move'.

NB: As you will have been gone for at least an hour from the office, the estimated distance you will have run, should anyone be annoying enough to ask, is 'at least 6K'.

You can actually carry on with all this being waited on hand-and-foot business for at least another day by simply pretending to have 'stiff legs'.

Joining a Slimming Club

Slimming clubs are a bit of a bore. All that calorie counting, weighing and steaming. Sharon lasted just one week at WeightWatchers before realising a single Frey Bentos pie would take up an entire day's points and she couldn't even have any mushy peas.

The trick is to get in, be a huge success and then quit immediately.

So, the night before your first day at the slimming club, we suggest you enjoy a full dinner nice and late. Drink alcohol as this will ensure you gain around 4lb in water retention. We recommend at least one bottle of wine. (If you're in AA, go for a big fat sticky toffee pudding instead.) On the day of your first weigh-in, go to the loo as little as possible and avoid anything like prunes, porridge or bran that may get things moving. Have a nice egg sandwich instead. Just before you enter the club you should drink at least half a litre of water. You should also wear as many layers of clothes as possible and all the jewellery that you own. This will ensure your maximum starter weight.

The following week, avoid booze for at least four days before the weigh-in. Eat nothing but prunes for breakfast and drink as little water as you can just before the meeting. Wear a light T-shirt or something in cheesecloth. You will find that with practically no effort at all you will have lost at least half a stone, will be basking in glory and hailed as a dieting hero.

Trust us on this. Sharon used this trick to great effect on the first week's weigh-in for *Celebrity Fit Club*.

Of course, after this, you never go again. Always leave on a high. If anyone asks you how your diet is going, always tell them you have 'joined a slimming club and lost half a stone'. After all, it's not as if you're telling a porky, is it?

Alternative Weight-loss Methods

All that running and weight-lifting does work – but it's a little dull. Here are some sure-fire everyday weight loss methods.

Buy cars without power steering: Simply drive around until you find really tight parking spots then spend half an hour straining at the steering wheel and you'll undergo the equivalent of a full workout as you park your car.

Turn the heating up: Whack the central heating up full strength and go to bed in your ski suit and thermals. You'll sweat out at least a pound a night.

Always have your watch ten minutes late: This will ensure you're always in a hurry. Spend your day stressed and rushing from one place to the next in a hurry. Tara manages this seamlessly. She's on New York time anyway.

Buy a penthouse: Remember the higher you go, the more you'll burn off staggering up to your flat at night. This is why supermodels never live in ground-floor flats. You can have any amount of hollandaise if you live in a penthouse.

Hang out with rugby teams: The boys are so big you'll automatically look small and thin next to them. If you can't find a rugby team then just join the slimming club, make friends with people who are bigger than you and hang out with them instead.

Hang out with Smug Couples: They always make you want to vomit (see page 115).

Use public transport in rush hour: We recommend the Northern line if you're in London. It's always packed and breaking down and you're guaranteed to emerge sweaty, stressed and thinner.

Order seafood all the time: If you're lucky, you'll get that dodgy oyster or the mussel that didn't open properly and should lose a stone over the next two hours.

A Word on Big Bottoms

The bottom line is to remember not to stress about your bottom. Some people are lucky with them. Some people just aren't.

Take Tara for example. Some days she eats nothing but Lion bars and Calypso ice lollies. And she's *never* been over a size eight and *never* had a filling. Whereas Sharon has been on a diet for the last ten years, owns twelve exercise videos and once spent an entire week fasting in a Thailand spa with a hose up her bottom pumping in cold coffee. And her bottom has never been as small as a size eight.

But one thing Sharon has learnt – as a former size sixteen – is this. There are lots of fads out there. There's the caveman diet of one meal a day, the diet where you just eat coconuts, the Beverly Hills where you just eat fruit, or the one where you just eat raw food. These might all work if you're a megastar who can stay horizontal for most of the day. But a naughty girl needs her calories for mischief.

Forget the fads. If you just drink a little less, steam the odd vegetable and move your bum a little more you'll lose the weight if you want to. Not that naughty. But the results are nice.

And, like we say, don't worry because it's probably not your fault. Sharon's run a marathon. Tara's sat on her sofa stuffing her face with chocolate and watching telly. Sharon is still fatter than Tara. Sometimes life just sucks that way.

CHECKLIST

✓ *Of course, celebrities don't bother with any of this. They just get their stomachs stapled. Google Anne Diamond for more information.*

Life is soooo much better when you're naughty

CONCLUSION:

How

Naughty

are

You?

PRAYER

*Grant me the serenity to accept I'm not alone in
thinking life sometimes sucks*

Courage to get my own back

*And the wisdom to realise that not everything
in this book is legal so I should always
watch out for CCTV.*

Have you been paying attention?

Where are you right now?

If you're reclining in your light-oatmeal cashmere socks which perfectly match the seats of the private jet you hitch-hiked on to, then well done. We're proud of you. If you're post-coital with a pop star and the socks are all you're wearing, then even better. You're our kind of harlot.

If you're just reading us on the loo, well, that's OK. Get out there and get on with it. If you're in an en suite then do follow our flushing etiquette tips before leaving.

If you've just found us on your boss's bedroom floor post-Christmas party, then the bad news is that you can't pull the sickie stunts. But having said that, a pay rise should be coming your way soon.

If you're in jail, we're sorry. But hey, just dab on the Carmex, find yourself a sexy lawyer and go and pull the forlorn but f***able stunt. Lawyers are always loaded. Plus, if we've any cash left after the boob jobs you could always ask if we'll spring your bail.

Life dumps on you sometimes. We all get dumped. By love, life, friends, work or family. Or a cruel trick of genetics that lands you with an incredibly flat chest. We've been there. Done that. You've just read the book we wrote.

As we said at the start, there's **no need for Miss Victim. We want Miss Vixen.** Even if they broke your heart, you should never let them break your will to get out there in killer heels. Never mind your hang-ups. Just go out and buy some hold-ups. Don't let people get on top of you. Get on top of them.

Life is what you make it. It's your own screenplay. And it's soooo much more fun to live life as a naughty girl. So what are you waiting for? Now, put us down. Get out there. Write yourself an X-rated scene for today and make sure you live it, you little strumpet.

Love,

Tara and Sharon

The Quiz

OK, it's time for your final maths test. Come on. **Step on the weighing scales of life**. Let's see how things add up. Fill in or circle your answer and we'll see how well you score on the next page.

WHICH OF THE FOLLOWING IS AN ACCEPTABLE LIGHT SNACK, WHILE STILL IN THE OFFICIAL GRIEVING PERIOD AFTER BEING DUMPED?

a) Nutritional and vitamin-enriched salad with walnut oil dressing. (*Is Gillian McKeith your flatmate or something? Come on, you're not trying hard enough.*) −1

b) Family-sized bucket of KFC. (*Perfectly healthy in your state.*) +2

c) Bottle of vodka, two Valiums and a slightly out-of-date block of Cheddar cheese you found in the back of the fridge at midnight, too hard to cut. (*Well, just this once, hey?*) +1

d) All of the above. (*Top marks.*) +3

TALKING OF THE OFFICIAL GRIEVING PERIOD, HAVE YOU
GOT THE HANG OF IT? SAY YOU STARTED DATING A MAN
ON OCTOBER 25ᵀᴴ AND HE DUMPED YOU ON BOXING DAY.
BY WHAT DATE SHOULD YOU BE OVER THE RELATIONSHIP?
Answer: New Year's Day will take you to the allowable ten per
cent period (*However, as the day before is a textbook snogging opportunity
and he's clearly a heel who was holding out for a Christmas present, we'd
prefer you to have pulled it together a bit earlier. A naughty girl's hurt
feelings should have been finished before the turkey was.*)
+1 if you answered New Year's Day, +3 if you said before that,
and −1 if you sulked for any longer.

WHAT UNDERWEAR ARE YOU WEARING RIGHT NOW? (WE
DID WARN YOU ABOUT THE SPOT CHECKS.)
a) Anything which has previously been boiled. (*Urgh.*) −1
b) Pop socks. (*Not unless you're Madonna in a pop video.*) −2
c) Last night's. You're just doing the walk of shame. (*Well done,
well done.*) +3

d) Silk knickers, in a light oatmeal which perfectly match the carpet of the private jet you've just hitch-hiked on to, and which the squillonaire pop star opposite you will be taking a closer look at soon. (*Well done. We hope it's just the one pop star, mind. Not the whole boyband. Remember, there's nothing in this game for three in a bed.*) +4

WHEN DID YOU LAST PHONE YOUR EX?

a) Let me just check 'Dialled numbers'. Oh dear. About three o'clock this morning. There appear to be some text messages too. (*We're disappointed. Delete his number and turn back to page 32.*) −4

b) Just a quick one to say you've no idea how that appalling rude message got on to his lawn. (*Well done.*) +2

c) You're just on your way over to his mother's to plead for her help and see if she can call him for you. (*Oh, please! Have you learnt nothing?*) −3

c) He's deleted from your phone. Obviously. Although his nightly sobbing pleas for a reunion are starting to do your head in. (*You've seen the light. We're proud.*) +3

HOW MUCH DO YOU SPEND ON SKINCARE PER WEEK? £____
This should be zero. You should be nicking the whole lot from
your flatmate. Delete one point for every pound you've spent.

HOW THOROUGHLY WAXED ARE YOU IN THE KNICKERS
DEPARTMENT?
a) I had a short back and sides done last week. (*Hmm.*) **−1**
b) Oh, I'll shave it when I get there. (*Oh, you lazy itchy cow.*) **−2**
c) I don't bother. Natural is best. (*Right. Still single by any chance?*) **−3**
d) I needed three shots of vodka and a
   Valium. They took that much off.
   (*Well done. Ideally, though, you should
   have been unconscious.*) **+3**

WHEN DID YOU LAST PULL?
a) Oh, this week. It was a Hollywood
   A-lister. You can read all about it in
   the *News of the World* this weekend,
   actually. (*Great, but we'd prefer a glossy
   cover. Still, well done.*) **+2**

b) I'm reading this in the back of a fire
   engine as we speak. And there's
   more than one hose I've got my eye
   on. (*Perfect. Go, girl, go! Really!*) **+3**
c) I've just woken up with my ex's
   father. (*Oh, well. He doesn't count under
   tart rules, we suppose.*) **+4**
d) I've given up men and joined a
   convent. (*Oh, for goodness' sake. We
   only wanted you to go there to pick up
   some vintage luggage.*) **−4**

WHO WAS THE LAST PERSON YOU SPOKE TO LAST NIGHT?

a) Ah. Now there's a tough question. Didn't, umm, quite catch the name. (*Well, you were in trauma so you're forgiven. And he doesn't count, does he?*) **+1**

b) Your shrink. (*Listen. It's much cheaper to just read us again.*) **−1**

c) The server at Burger King. (*Acceptable, as long as you were late-night comfort eating within your allotted ten per cent sulking time, post-break-up. However, if the server is the ski instructor who followed you home from your holiday, then we did warn you to give a fake address.*) **0**

d) Your AA sponsor. (*Well done. If you've overdone the choccy cake a bit thanks to us, then we recommend you do a quick re-read of the diet section.*) **+2**

WHAT ARE YOU WEARING ON YOUR FEET?

a) Fishnet hold-ups. And I'm horizontal. (*Good girl.*) **+4**

b) Orthopaedic Dr Scholls, with tights in a 'flesh' colour. (*We give up.*) **−6**

c) Killer heels with red soles. (*Perfect. And we don't mind if they're genuine Louboutins or you painted the soles. Both are acceptable.*) **+5**

d) Nothing. Valentino really objects to people wearing shoes on his yacht. (*Oh! Well done, you!*) +10

Final Scores

20+ Congratulations! You are a fully fledged member of the Naughty Girl's Club and it's a pleasure having you on board. Now, send us an invitation should you ever decide to get married and we promise not to snigger if you turn up in white.

11–20 Well. OK. At least you're not shutting yourself away wimpering to Sinéad O'Connor and sulking any more. But you know, you could be getting away with so much more. Pull a sickie next week and stay in and read us.

1–10 Was it the tights that dragged your score down? Look, if it's just wardrobe issues there's hope for you yet. But otherwise you have to stop being so well behaved. We haven't been good for years.

O or below If you're not going to pay us any attention we're just wasting our time. Go back to the beginning and read us again. In heels this time.

Movie Choices in Times of Crisis

Deciding what to watch when you're sitting on your own in a foul mood is crucial. The last thing you want to see is a love story, thin people, and all-round happiness when your own life sucks. So here are some carefully vetted movie plots.

Titanic Good-looking rich man who has proposed turns out to be psycho. Boat sinks, and most people die including new, perfect love. Girl is left alone. Proves you don't need money. And that those girls who are engaged, young, rich and beautiful are probably really miserable.

Last Tango in Paris Woman meets good-looking stranger for amazing sex after finding perfect apartment with very reasonable rent. He turns out to be married (albeit to newly dead wife). Proves that getting gazumped can be a good thing. And that if you were ignored by a handsome man it's probably for the best. Oh. And that leaving your butter out of the fridge overnight is not necessarily a bad thing.

Charlie and the Chocolate Factory Advocates eating large amounts of chocolate and contains no sex. Also good if your fake tan goes wrong. You can always play along and pretend to be an Oompa Loompa for the evening.

Terminator II Attractive perfect man is actually a robot. Proves perfect man is unlikely to exist. And if he does he may well be from the future and want to kill you.

Shallow Hal Man is conned into believing robustly built girl is actually skinny. Finds out the truth. Falls in love with her anyway. Moral: it doesn't matter if you don't make it to the gym.

Splash Girl who is half-fish gets man. Moral: hey. Don't get down about your looks.

Thelma and Louise Even after meeting Brad Pitt, the girls still have a lousy day and end up driving off a cliff. Moral: handsome men don't solve things.

Pretty Woman It doesn't matter if you have been a complete slut all your life. You can still pull a rich good-looking man.

AND DON'T WATCH . . .

Love, Actually Avoid like the plague. In fact, avoid any film by Richard Curtis, there's a very good chance it'll be *unbearably* smug.

Directory

These numbers may come in useful.

AA:

- Alcoholics Anonymous: In the United Kingdom and Ireland, look for 'Alcoholics Anonymous' in any telephone directory. In most urban areas, a telephone service staffed mainly by volunteer AA members will be happy to answer your questions and/or put you in touch with those who can. Or you can write to:
  Alcoholics Anonymous
  PO Box 1
  10 Toft Green
  York YO1 7ND
  Tel: 01904 644026
  Outside the UK, please contact the General Service office nearest to you.
- The one that does car breakdowns: www.theaa.com

Airlines:

- BA: www.britishairways.com
- Virgin: www.virgin-atlantic.com
- As the others have never upgraded us, they don't count

Botox: Dr Sebag: 020 7637 0548

Agent Provocateur: www.agentprovocateur.com

Amazon: www.amazon.co.uk

Big knickers: Spanx: www.spanx.com

Buckingham Palace: www.royal.gov.uk

Cakes: Jane Asher: 020 7584 6177

Carmex: www.carmex.co.uk

Chocolate: Charbonnel et Walker champagne truffles: 020 7491 0939 (nothing else will do)

Darphin: Paris: 020 7409 6700 (fabulous skincare)

Elton John fan club: www.eltonjohn.com

Eve Lom: www.evelom.co.uk

Feng Shui:

- www.fengshuidoctor.co.uk
- www.russellgrant.com

George Michael fan club: www.georgemichael.com

Google: www.google.co.uk

Guerlain: 020 7235 5059 (Midnight Secret)

Hair (hairdressers too good to shag):
- Daniel Galvin: www.danielgalvin.com, 020 7486 9661
- Richard Ward: 020 7730 1222

Harrods: www.harrods.com, 020 7730 1234

Harvey Nicks: www.harveynichols.com

Hats – via Philip Treacy: www.philiptreacy.co.uk, 020 7730 3992

Heat magazine: heat@emap.com

Hello magazine: www.hellomagazine.com

Help the Aged: www.helptheaged.org.uk

Hosiery: MyTights.com do next-day delivery for emergency break-up stocking requests. (Mind you, don't actually buy any tights.)

Karin Herzog: www.karinherzog.co.uk (the moisturiser is perfect for post-heavy-drinking break-ups. Get your flatmate some for Christmas.)

La Perla: www.laperla.com (perfectly reasonable 'I'm sorry' gifts)

Legal Aid: www.legalservices.gov.uk

Liposuction: Check they're a member of the British Association of Aesthetic Plastic Surgeons (www.baaps.org.uk) before going ahead

Louboutin: www.christianlouboutin.fr, we love those little shoes!

Louis Vuitton: www.louisvuitton.com

Manolo Blahnik: www.manoloblahnik.com

Martini: www.martini.com

Myla: www.myla.com/uk/

NA: www.ukna.org (good luck!)

OK! Magazine: www.ok-magazine.co.uk
(in the US: www.ok-magazine.com, 212 672 0800)

Prada: www.prada.com

Press Complaints Commission (if they're stalking you and your celebrity boyfriend too much): 0845 600 2757

Rehab Centres:
- The Priory: 01372 860 400
- The Meadows: 928 684 3926

Restaurants (where the waiters will pass messages to sexy men for you):
- The Ivy: 020 7836 4751
- Le Caprice: 020 7629 2239
- San Lorenzo: 020 7584 1074
- The Wolseley: 020 7499 6996

Robbie Williams Fan Club: www.robbiewilliams.com

Rugby Team Fixtures: www.rfu.com

Selfridges: www.selfridges.com (where you can buy more gorgeous skincare like Decleor)

STD clinics: www.ssha.info/public/clinics/index.asp

Stomach stapling: Oh, just Google Anne Diamond

Threshers: www.threshergroup.com

Vivienne Westwood: www.viviennewestwood.co.uk, 020 7924 4747

WeightWatchers: www.weightwatchers.co.uk

The

Naughty

Girl's Guide

to Saying

Thank You

We'd like to thank Mara at San Lorenzo's where it all began over a Costoletta Milanese and a few tears. Tara had just broken up with her boyfriend, now very good friend, Jamie, whom she'd also like to thank. In the aftermath of that dark time, she was able to find a sense of humour and be inspired to put pen to paper. Sharon was dumped three weeks later and we suppose we ought to thank that little loser, too. Or at least apologise for the state of his lawn.

We've drawn from life's mistakes and from adventures and experiences we have shared with our friends. We'd like to thank those who have always been there for us in times of life's emergencies. In particular, Tara's great friend Isabella Blow, who sadly passed away this year (knowing Issy she'd definitely get her hands on a copy even though she's in heaven. In fact she's probably already read it. She always managed to get handbags before they'd even been designed). She was one of the ultimate naughty girls!

Thank you to Robyn Neild and Sian Rance – we love the artwork and design you've done for the book – and everyone else who helped make it happen and didn't come up with any excuses about burgled flats to get it all done in time. Thanks for the help and support of Gordon Wise at Curtis Brown, Antonia Hodgson at Little, Brown Book Group, and Becca Barr at Stuart Higgins Communications. You've all been fantastic.

We'd like to thank Darphin because all naughty girls need good serums for their face. Not forgetting Richard Ward Hair and Metro Spa where a lot of this book was written whilst having a pedicure!

And finally we'd like to thank our families for putting up with our naughty girl behaviour. Sharon's parents for allowing us to print some of the finer details which they weren't previously aware of. And Tara's mother who wisely edited out some of our even naughtier confessions.

We've left these last pages blank for all the phone numbers you naughty girls are bound to collect, now you've got our fabulous tips safely under your suspender belts. And we don't mind if you deface our lovely book by stapling in extra pages.

Well, what are you waiting for?

_____

_____

_____

_____

_____

_____

_____

_____

_____

_____

_____

_____

_____
_____
_____
_____
_____
_____
_____
_____
_____
_____
_____
_____
_____
_____
_____
_____
_____
_____
_____
_____
_____
_____
_____
_____